# Who Needs a
# Superhero?

## Finding Virtue, Vice, and What's Holy in the Comics

# H. Michael Brewer

BakerBooks
Grand Rapids, Michigan

Published by Baker Books
a division of Baker Publishing Group
P.O. Box 6287, Grand Rapids, MI 49516-6287
www.bakerbooks.com

Printed in the United States of America

**To Janet,
my Wonder Woman**

Library of Congress Cataloging-in-Publication Data
Brewer, H. Michael, 1954–
    Who needs a superhero? : finding virtue, vice, and what's holy in the comics /
H. Michael Brewer.
       p.     cm.
    Includes bibliographical references.
    ISBN 0-8010-6510-0 (pbk.)
    1. Comic books, strips, etc.—Religious aspects.  I. Title.
PN6712.B74  2004
741.5′.09—dc22
                                               2004013963

# Contents

# Foreword

# Superheroes in the Making

When I was twelve years old, I was a paperboy for one reason: I needed money to buy comic books. I loved those pamphlet-sized, 35- to 70-cent, four-color wonders printed on cheap newsprint.

I especially identified with Spider-Man, who was a superhero, yes, but also a young adult trying to cope with underachievement and disappointment. If I was having a bad day, Spider-Man's was even worse. If I got a low grade on a class report, Peter Parker could best me by losing his job at the *Daily Bugle* for turning in blurred pictures of Spider-Man's skirmish with Doc Ock, catching the blame of New York City for the latest round of power outages, and failing every course at Empire University because he missed too many classes.

The comics also awakened my first spiritual stirrings. As I told syndicated columnist Terry Mattingly in a recent interview, people are always looking for answers to the big questions, like "What am I doing here?" I was no exception, only comic books did a better job of giving me answers than many of the sermons I heard from priests and preachers. Comics hooked me with living color and fast-paced action, framing a fantastical world of good and evil where I could witness how courage, the exercising of one's unique gifts, and divine intervention could save the day.

Comics seemed to whisper of God's plan for humanity, and gradually I began to see Jesus as the ultimate superhero. He created the universe. He became the God-man, with amazing abilities and powers beyond mere mortals. On earth he commanded the weather, cast out demons, raised the dead. Like other heroes, he came from humble beginnings and grew up with surrogate parents, Mary and Joseph (think Ma and Pa Kent, or Aunt May and Uncle Ben). He became renowned for standing up for truth and justice, and performed amazing feats like changing water to wine or telling off the establishment by saying even outcasts like prostitutes would make it into heaven before them. Like Spider-Man or Batman, Jesus was considered a menace to authorities. He had skirmishes with humankind's greatest enemy, Satan, the first villain to plot world domination. As mirrored by the great superhero stories, even friends abandoned Jesus at the hour of his sacrifice.

Still, Jesus urged his followers not to rise up and destroy the empire by force, but rather to pray for good and repay ill will with kindness. He told us how to become new creatures, promising someday we would be transformed and able to do the things he could.

The world is more chaotic than ever, and evil seems as evident and powerful as any comic book villain. There really are people hell-bent on world domination, authorities set on destroying entire populations, terrorists who crash planes into towers to murder thousands. Another generation may find human cloning a reality, along with dark predictions that these clones will be used as slaves. There still looms the threat of a madman who, by accessing computer codes, could take over nuclear systems internationally and plunge the world into nuclear catastrophe.

No wonder superheroes are more popular today than ever and movies based on comic books are wildly successful. In a dark and sinister world that leads us to believe we're insignificant, we need to know we were created for something greater. We need to be pushed to strive for big ideals and bigger dreams. We need the thrilling promise that we all have the potential to be superheroes.

The truth is God transformed himself to save the world, and as coheirs to the kingdom of God, Christians are given the ability to help shape it. Christ promised the Christian great power. And as comic book legend Stan Lee is oft-quoted, "with great power, comes great responsibility," which echoes the words of Jesus: "From everyone who has been given much, much will be demanded" (Luke 12:48). We must not forget our status as world shapers and the great responsibility we bear. In discussing his reason for making *The Passion of the Christ*, Mel Gibson said one of the definitions of *truth* in Greek is "unforgetting." We need superheroes to remind us that the story isn't over, that there is work to be done.

It's a good thing that H. Michael Brewer remembers his childhood heroes in comic books. In doing so, he remembers God and his message for us.

Leo Partible
Filmmaker
Los Angeles

7

# Introduction
# Funny Books, Serious Questions

I have issues.

Thousands of issues.

I store them alphabetically in plastic bags to keep them in mint condition.

I'm talking about my collection of comic books, of course. I've been collecting for forty years. I love it when someone looks at me oddly and wonders aloud why a grown man reads "funny books."

Sometimes I explain about the unique art form of words and pictures combining to create something bigger than either. Other times I launch into the "some-cultures-respect-comic-books-as-entertainment-for-all-ages" speech. If nothing else fazes my questioner, I'll mention that a near-mint copy of *X-Men* #1 recently sold for $45,000 and watch a jaw drop.

All that is true as far as it goes, but none of it adequately explains my weekly pilgrimage to the local comic shop. I'll come clean with you. I read comics because I love heroes.

I'm not alone in my admiration for heroes. Those noble champions are the heart of our television programs, our movies, and our best-sellers. A list of humanity's greatest stories and legends is a roll call of heroes: Gilgamesh, Hercules, Beowulf, El Cid, Roland, Arthur, and Robin Hood. The names and outward trappings may change, but each generation creates its own heroes: Sherlock Holmes, Nick Carter, the Shadow, Doc Savage, James Bond, Frodo Baggins, Mr. Spock, Indiana Jones, Neo.

We live in a scary world, and hero stories express our longing for safety and security. While we can sometimes hedge ourselves against disaster, life is ultimately beyond our control. *If only some more-than-human power would set the world right,* we think. *If only someone could walk beside us to see us through the perils of life, someone genuinely good and supremely strong.*

So we keep looking for heroes. We idolize our athletes, but they scarcely make any real difference in the world. We elevate our leaders on lofty pedestals, but from that vantage their clay feet are all the more obvious. We expect miracles from doctors, cops, and firefighters, but they fail us often enough to remind us that they too are only human, after all.

When real heroes let us down, we turn to the fictional variety. The more troubling our times, it seems, the grander our heroes. In these days of terrorism, war, epidemics, ecological disaster, and shaky economies, we need superheroes, those costumed do-gooders who were born in the frightful shadows of the Great Depression and World War II.

Today the monthly adventures of thousands of superheroes published by dozens of companies have evolved into the most elaborate mythology in the world—and I love the stories. I love superheroes' costumes and powers, their origins and convoluted plots, their nobility, their heroism, and even their foibles, struggles, temporary defeats, and eventual victories.

Admittedly, not all superheroes offer sterling role models. Like television, movies, and books in general, the comic book field has its share of needless violence, sexual stereotypes, and other offensive material. But if we separate the wheat from the chaff, we'll find comic books offering as much heroism, idealism, and sacrificial nobility as any area of the entertainment industry.

In fact, nobody does heroes better than comic books. As far as I can see, there's just one drawback with these caped adventurers: they aren't real.

That leaves us in a bind. Flesh-and-blood heroes aren't big enough to save us, and comic book heroes are make-believe. Fortunately our fictional heroes point beyond themselves to someone both real and super.

If you think this discussion is taking a religious turn, you're right. The spiritual hunger for heroes is woven into the fabric of the human creature. Our Maker built us with a persistent longing for a rescuer who will save us from injustice and suffering. We dream of a champion who will lift us and lead us home. In our bleakest moments, we pray for someone to save us from ourselves.

Religion is the deepest expression of our longing for a savior, but all our hero stories finally point in the same direction. Every heroic saga, legend, and myth is ultimately a variation on one universal story: When all seemed lost, a hero stepped in to rescue us from the evil around and within us. As it turns out, this story happens to be true, and the hero is absolutely real.

Come along with me and I'll show you. I'll be your tour guide for sightseeing in Batman's Gotham City, Thor's Asgard, and points beyond. We'll be visiting dangerous territory. Insurance is required. Capes are optional. Wherever we end up, I guarantee we'll have fun getting there.

# 1 Superman
# The Saving Son from Above

L ook! Up in the sky! It's a bird! It's a plane! It's . . ."
You finished that line from memory, didn't you? That's a tribute to the enduring popularity of Superman, the first and still greatest comic book superhero of them all. The star of comic books, novels, radio, cartoons, television, and movies, the man from Krypton in his bold red cape may well be the most recognizable figure on the planet. Even people who have never opened a comic book in their lives know about Superman.

I found this out one evening when, on the job as a pastor, I was handing out bulletins and welcoming folks to a community Thanksgiving service. In my lapel was a small pin featuring the triangular red and gold S of Superman's insignia. I hadn't worn the pin to make a statement. On my way to worship, I'd thrown on the first sport coat within reach without noticing the Superman symbol.

11

Everyone else noticed, though. I endured some good-natured joshing about my secret identity being out of the bag, and could I really leap tall steeples in a single bound? Half the worshipers that night commented on my Superman lapel pin, but not everyone approved of such frivolity from a man of the cloth.

One dour-faced woman shook her head and said to me, "I know that can't be what it looks like."

She stared at the Superman insignia, her forehead furrowed and mouth pinched. After a moment her face relaxed and she said, "I know! The S stands for Savior."

"Not exactly, ma'am," I replied.

Again the wrinkled brow as she said, "It must stand for Son of God."

I shook my head.

"Then what does it mean?" she asked with exasperation.

I tried my softest, most pastoral voice, wanting to break it to her gently: "The S stands for Superman."

The poor woman drew herself ramrod straight and radiated disapproval, but I leaned forward and added in a conspiratorial whisper, "And Superman stands for Jesus."

## A Hero of Global Proportions

Is it true? Does the strange visitor from another planet really represent the saving Son of God?

That's probably not what teenagers Jerry Siegel and Joe Shuster had in mind when they created Superman more than sixty years ago. Siegel and Shuster, second-generation Jewish immigrants, attended high school together in Cleveland. There the boys dreamed up the idea that would become Superman. They envisioned a larger-than-life figure from another planet with superhuman powers and abilities.

While Nazi Germany touted the Aryan "super-man" as a symbol of subjugation and conquest, Siegel and Shuster imagined a hero who would use his powers to defend the weak and uphold justice. Joe Shuster, the artist in the team, dressed their character in a bright red and blue costume inspired by science fiction pulp covers. They dubbed him Superman, slapped a big *S* on his chest, and tried to sell the idea to publishers.

The publishing world was underwhelmed by the visitor from Krypton. Siegel and Shuster wanted to sell Superman as a newspaper comic strip but couldn't break into the field. As a compromise, the Cleveland creators packaged several strips into a short story and sold it to DC Comics.

In those days, comic books consisted mostly of reprints from newspaper strips or original action stories featuring spies, explorers, cowboys, detectives, and science fiction adventurers. The red-and-blue brainchild of two Ohio teens utterly changed the face of the young comic book industry.

In 1938 Superman exploded onto the newsstand in *Action Comics* #1. On the cover Superman hoisted a car over his head while villains fled in panic. The editor nearly replaced the cover art, fearing readers would find the whole idea preposterous. His worries were unfounded. America loved Superman. The first issue of *Action Comics* sold 200,000 issues. By issue #7, circulation reached half a million. In 1939 DC launched a second comic book for the character, this one titled *Superman*. Radio programs, cartoons, and an endless array of licensed products were just around the corner.

In the original version Superman was a tough-talking hero with bulletproof skin and incredible strength. He didn't fly but traveled by immense eighth-of-a-mile leaps. He was rough on bad guys and always showed up just in time to rescue the innocent victims of crime and oppression.

13

The plotline for his story is simple enough too. On the doomed planet Krypton, scientist Jor-El places his son Kal-El in a prototype rocket and blasts him into space. As the rocket departs, massive earthquakes tear Krypton apart. Little Kal-El, hurtling through the void, is the sole survivor and last son of Krypton. The rocket crashes in a Kansas wheat field, where an elderly couple finds the uninjured baby. Ma and Pa Kent receive the boy as a gift from above and raise him as their own, naming him Clark Kent. When Clark grows up, he demonstrates powers and abilities that set him apart from mere mortals. Eventually Clark Kent leaves Smallville and moves to Metropolis, where he works as a reporter for a major newspaper. Once in Metropolis, the man from Krypton maintains a double identity: meek and mild reporter Clark Kent and dauntless hero Superman.

Juvenile? Preposterous? Even the most devoted comic book fans will admit that this is not Pulitzer Prize material. Yet something in Superman strikes a chord deep within many hearts. For some reason we resonate with this gaudy character.

What is there about Superman that's made him a star of global proportions?

## Man of Steel, Son of Earth

From the very beginning, and through all the changes over the decades, Superman's mission was clear: to save the world.

Whether intentional, accidental, or providential, the parallels between the Kryptonian's beginnings and those of Jesus are undeniable. Let's look at these profound similarities to the Galilean that lie deeply embedded in the story and character of Superman.

14

A promotional blurb for the 1978 Superman movie sounds almost scriptural: "Marlon Brando as Jor-El, who gave his only son to save the world . . ."[1]

Superman arrives in this world as Kal-El, who comes from the heavens, sent by his father to a planet desperately in need of his help. In the same manner, Jesus is sent from heaven by his Father. Both babies arrive miraculously, one by rocket ship, the other through a virgin birth.

Great danger attends both advents: exploding planets and crashing rockets in Superman's case; Herod's murderous soldiers in Jesus's case.

Joseph and Mary welcome Jesus. They are good, pious, working-class people who recognize this unlikely arrival as a gift from God. Like the Kents, Joseph and Mary raise their mystery child as if he were their own, but in fact he belongs to the world. Jesus grows up in small-town obscurity, and when he reaches manhood he leaves Nazareth and makes his way eventually to Jerusalem, the ancient metropolis, where his destiny awaits him.

Sound familiar?

More parallels can be seen in each man's story: On the way to Jerusalem, Jesus reveals powers that set him apart from others. He works wonders no one else can. He walks on the surface of the sea. He commands the weather. He turns water into wine. Yet his unearthly power is tempered by sheer goodness. He uses his power not for his own gain but for the sake of people in need. He casts out demons, gives sight to the blind, feeds the hungry, heals every kind of illness, and even raises the dead.

Power is probably the most distinctive quality associated with Superman in the popular mind. The extent of Superman's abilities has yo-yoed through the years, depending upon the whims of writers and the dictates of editors. The Man of Steel probably hit his peak in the 1960s when he pushed around planets. The old guy isn't quite so formidable these days, but neither is he a pushover: Superman flies at supersonic speeds, lifts airliners without breaking a sweat, is invulnerable to attack by any conventional weapon (even nuclear arms), can see molecules and distant planets with equal clarity, and peers through mountains or vaporizes steel girders with a single glance.

Traditionally, Superman has only two absolute weaknesses: magic and Kryptonite. He operates in a scientific world and is undone by magical acts that defy natural law. And when Superman's native planet exploded, the fragments were converted into a radioactive mineral that is deadly to him. Even in the world of comic book "reality," magic is rare, and Kryptonite is harder to find than a mint copy of *Action Comics* #1. For all practical purposes, Superman is invincible and unstoppable.

A thoughtful reading of the Superman saga raises two unavoidable questions about the character. If Superman is really that powerful, why doesn't he rule the world? And if Superman is really that good (a question tackled more in chapter 5), why doesn't he save the world?

Frankly, any thoughtful observer of life will inevitably ask similar questions about Jesus Christ. If Jesus is as powerful and loving as the Bible describes him, why is the world in such a mess? If Jesus truly reigns, as the church claims, why do suffering and injustice still loom so large in the human story? Our discussion of Superman will shed some light on the problem.

## To Use or Lose the Power

Imagine the temptation to exercise omnipotence in a world of mere mortals. In an amusing story by John Byrne, Superman's archenemy Lex Luthor programs a computer to unravel the connection between Superman and Clark Kent. When the computer reveals that Superman and Kent are one and the same, Luthor utterly rejects the idea. The authority-hungry Luthor cannot conceive that someone with Superman's powers would pose as an ordinary man and work for a living. Luthor speaks for the world at large when he says, "I know that no man with the power of Superman would ever pretend to be a mere human! Such power is to be constantly exploited! Such power is to be used!"[2]

Could Luthor's reasoning be true? Why work when you can simply seize anything you want? Why be a friend when you can be a tyrant? Why serve others when they can be forced to serve you?

Early in his career Superman does indeed wrestle with the dilemma of irresistible power. He realizes no earthly authority can possibly restrain him, so he imposes his own limits. He agrees to abide by the laws of the land ("the American way") and establishes a personal code against taking human life. Acknowledging the potential risk inherent in his own power, Superman turns for help to Batman, another costumed crime fighter. Superman entrusts to Batman a rare piece of Kryptonite, which Batman guards as a fail-safe weapon—a contingency for the day when Superman may, as Luthor speculates, abuse his powers and harm the very people he's sworn to protect.

Both caped heroes realize that only Batman is sufficiently resourceful and ruthless enough to bring down Superman; if necessary, Batman will destroy Superman to protect innocents. This is precisely why Superman chooses Batman to hold the Kryptonite. The Man of Steel makes himself utterly vulnerable for the sake of those he's come to save.

In a different storyline Superman faces three criminals from his native Krypton. These outlaws inherited

17

the same powers as Superman but have used them to murder the population of an entire planet. Worst of all, they committed this unspeakable atrocity for no reason. They are not seeking safety, wealth, domination, or even revenge. They incinerate cities for sport. They revel in mass murder. When Superman confronts the unrepentant killers, they laugh about the horrors they've perpetrated.

Even if Superman can somehow triumph over these three foes, he realizes no prison can hold them. No matter what safeguards he uses, eventually these murderers will break free and continue their monstrous crimes. Faced with an insoluble dilemma, Superman takes an action he will never again repeat. He declares himself to be a legal representative of his birth planet, draws a piece of Kryptonite from a lead container, shields himself from the deadly radiation, and exposes the criminals to the lethal substance.

The Kryptonian renegades die slowly. Superman has ample time to reconsider his choice, but he stays the course. He brandishes the Kryptonite until the last criminal is dead. As he stands over their bodies, Superman vows that he will never again take a human life.

Years later, Superman is still haunted by the execution. Eventually he consults a psychiatrist for help to deal with his guilt.

The story reveals Superman's uprightness and profound respect for life. Batman and Kryptonite notwithstanding, the world's chief protection against the power of Superman is his simple goodness. Unlike Luthor, Superman genuinely cares about others, and he views his power as a responsibility for service, not an opportunity for exploitation.

It's a theme in the stories of superheroes that the world still grapples with believing.

# Made to Save

The Gospel account of Luke says that in preparation for ministry, Jesus enters the Judean wilderness, where for forty days he fasts, prays, and wrestles with temptation. When Jesus is hungry, the devil tempts him to turn stones into bread. But Jesus will not use his power for his own comfort.

Next the devil offers to Jesus all the kingdoms of the world, if Jesus will merely worship Satan. This would mean using power as Satan would, as the world does—to rule and control. Jesus turns from the devil's offer. Jesus has come to serve, not to be served.

Finally the devil urges Jesus to demonstrate his power by flinging himself from the pinnacle of the temple in downtown Jerusalem. Surely after a public display of such invincibility, the devil reasons, the crowds will beg to follow Jesus. But Christ again refuses the easy way. He will use his power to help people, not to compel, dazzle, or coerce.

Jesus returns from the wilderness and turns his attention and energy to healing, having forsworn the use of his power for personal advantage. The fullness of God's omnipotence lives in Jesus, but he willingly lays it aside to live in a human world. He is almighty but will make himself as vulnerable as any other man or woman.

# Connecting the Celestial-to-Clay Dots

More than power and goodness link Jesus and Superman. Each leads a double life and goes by many names that explain their respective natures.

Kal-El is both Clark Kent and Superman. Neither persona is a disguise or a pretense. Each face is true; one cannot be separated from the other. Superman really is the son of Ma and Pa Kent, just as surely as he's the last son of Krypton. Having grown up on earth, Superman understands human problems and needs, yet he brings into our world more-than-human possibilities.

Jesus also embodies this dual nature. He's both a carpenter from Galilee and the Redeemer from heaven, the Son of Man and Son of God. Jesus isn't sometimes one and then the other. He's always both. Theologians explain that Jesus is fully human and fully God—one of us and yet . . . not. He's tempted as we are, yet he doesn't sin. He has needs, but those needs never blind him to the needs of others. He's both the perfect image of God and the untarnished image of humanity as we were meant to be.

Superman's Kryptonian name, Kal-El, offers interesting and unexpected insight into this dual nature of Jesus. Take a look: *Kal* is a given name, the Kryptonian equivalent of a first name. *El* is the surname, the true name; *El* is the name Superman shares with his father Jor-El. *El* is also the Hebrew word for God. The word occurs thousands of times in the Old Testament, sometimes in the longer form, *Elohim*, and often combined with other words and names.

Who knows if Jerry Siegel or Joe Shuster intended the Hebrew meaning of El when they named their character, but that final connection confirms for me what I told the woman at the Thanksgiving service: Superman really does stand for Jesus, who comes from the world above, sent by his Father, bearing both his Father's name and nature. Of course Jesus can do things no one else can do! Who else but Jesus could reconcile God and humanity? No wonder Matthew refers to the newborn Jesus as Emmanuel, a name that means "God is with us" or more literally "El is with us."

The name Emmanuel captures the ironic grace of Jesus's life. He comes from above us but stands beside us. That can't be said of many powerful people who love to stand above the crowd—conquerors, intellectuals, moneymakers, celebrities, athletes, and politicians. To what extent do merely mortal power brokers spend their time looking down on others instead of looking around for opportunities to serve? To what degree will they leave the world better for having been here?

Surely Superman stands apart from today's powerful people. He explains in a conversation with Wonder Woman, "I think the best way to effect meaningful change is to work alongside people, rather than above them. At least, it's always worked for me."[3]

If Krypton had never exploded and Superman had remained on the planet of his birth, he could have lived an idyllic existence in a techno-utopia. But in doing so he never would have made a difference in our world. Only in coming to earth is Superman able to accomplish his saving work among mortals. He cannot save us from a distance.

Possibly God could have found a less costly means of saving us. He might have rescued us from on high, aloof and untouched by the mud and blood of human existence, but in fact God chose to accomplish our salvation down here. Christ stepped down from the heavens and joined us in our earthbound humanity.

## Saving by Heart

A now classic episode of the television sitcom *Seinfeld* shows Jerry and George arguing about the extent of Superman's powers. Jerry insists that Superman's arsenal of powers surely includes a super sense of humor. He argues that if Superman has super hearing, super vision, and super breath, then a super sense of humor must follow.

21

George is skeptical. He asserts that Superman's powers are all physical. Super is only skin-deep and does not apply to the inner man.

The debate is one the comic book writers danced around for decades. One of their favorite ploys has been to strip Superman of his more-than-human abilities temporarily. In the process they've revealed that even a non-super Superman is still a hero. For instance, when Superman is depowered and shrunken to doll size by the robotic villain Brainiac, the diminutive champion decoys the murderous Brainiac while Lois Lane and Jimmy Olsen escape. When Superman battles the Parasite, he fights on even after his powers have been absorbed by his foe. And when Superman visits the city of Kandor, whose atmosphere renders him utterly mortal and vulnerable, the Man of Steel dubs himself Nightwing and adopts a new identity as a costumed do-gooder—without the help of special powers.

Dozens of similar stories depict a humbled Superman who continues to save the weak and defend the underdog. So on this point, George is wrong and Jerry is right, at least in principle: Superman's greatness does extend into the spiritual realm. While invulnerability and super strength are undeniable assets, Superman's heroism is ultimately rooted in his heart, not his biceps.

Yes, if ever a story showed us how heroism is rooted in the heart, it might be Superman's. But as I told the woman at that Thanksgiving service, my Superman is found in Jesus, whose supreme act of salvation was accomplished through weakness and his willingness to bow his head to death.

Flying in the face of first-century Jewish expectations, Jesus did not arrive at the head of an invincible angelic army. Instead, he was born in a stable, lived in poverty, bore the contempt of Israel's leaders, died in humiliation, and was laid in a borrowed tomb. In the final showdown with evil, he did not rescue us through such superhuman powers as commanding storms or quelling demons. Jesus saved us by the love of his heart, the love that embraced the cross and entered the tomb for our sake.

The similarities between Superman and Jesus are myriad, yet the story of the man who came down from Krypton is the palest shadow of the story of the man who came down from heaven. Laying aside celestial glory, Jesus cast his lot with humanity and joined us in the pain and turmoil of human life. He was with us in the first century, and he is here with us still, beside us now and always.

Superman's motto is "Up, up, and away," but perhaps the mission of Jesus is better caught in these words: "Down, down to stay."

Thank God.

# 2 The Hulk
# The Monster Within

A "brutal, bestial mockery of a human—that creature which fears nothing—which despises reason and worships power!"[1]

"A savage, marauding monster from some mad nether world. . . ."[2]

"The most dangerous living creature on earth. . . ."[3]

Believe it or not, these words describe one of the most durable superheroes of the past forty years. Brutal. Bestial. Savage. Marauding. Most dangerous. This doesn't sound like a hero to you?

You're right. The Hulk is truly a repulsive brute, and his story is ugly. In fact, nearly the only note of heroism in the Hulk's tragic tale is sounded in the events of his origin.

Envision somewhere in the New Mexico desert a staging ground for the most destructive weapon ever created. In a shielded bunker, Dr. Bruce Banner prepares to test the bomb he masterminded. The soft-spoken Banner is a brilliant scientist, the only man in the world who understands the physics behind the gamma bomb. With the flick of a switch, he begins the countdown for the detonation.

But with the seconds ticking by, Banner is horrified to see a teenager drive casually onto the testing grounds.

"Stop the countdown!" Banner orders and rushes from the bunker. He leaps into a military jeep, punches the key into the ignition, and stamps his foot on the accelerator to roar across the open desert, where he yanks the boy from his jalopy.

"The kids bet me I wouldn't have nerve to sneak past the guards," admits the teenager, a boy named Rick Jones.

Banner drags the lad over the sand and shoves him into a trench. Unfortunately, Banner's envious colleague in the bunker has done nothing to delay the detonation of the bomb. This is an opportunity to do away with his brilliant superior and steal his work. Before Banner can join Rick Jones in the trench, the gamma bomb explodes, saturating the scientist in raw gamma radiation.

Bruce Banner doesn't die, but within a few hours the wretched man will bitterly regret his survival. That evening when the last rays of the sun disappear behind the horizon, Banner grows feverish and sick. His head throbs. His clothing rips into tatters as the meek scientist transforms into the incredible Hulk.

The first glimpse of the Hulk shocks the reader. True to his name, the Hulk towers head and shoulders over normal human beings. His arms and legs are as thick as tree trunks and more powerful than pile drivers. Beneath a wild thatch of hair, the creature's corpse-gray face recalls the Frankenstein monster. The story captions declare the Hulk to be the most powerful man on earth. While the designation of "man" might be challenged, his power is unquestionable. Within the first two pages of his comic book existence, the Hulk smashes through a brick wall, crushes a jeep, and overpowers a squad of armed soldiers. At dawn the Hulk reverts to Bruce Banner, but we are assured that the juggernaut will return at nightfall.

At first the Hulk is merely confused and brutish, like a force of nature unleashed on an unsuspecting world. Soon, however, the Hulk grows bitter and angry. By issue #2, after capturing a spaceship of alien invaders, the Hulk muses, "With this flying dreadnought under me, I can wipe out all mankind!"

A few pages later in the same story, Bruce Banner's love interest, Betty Ross, asks the Hulk, "Who are you? Why do you hate us so?"

The Hulk replies with characteristic venom, "Hate you? Why shouldn't I hate you? Why shouldn't I hate all mankind? Look what men have done to me!"

If any doubt is left as to the villainous status of the lumbering destroyer, the writer describes the Hulk as the "foe of every human being on earth."[4]

The Hulk himself confirms this repeatedly. For instance, after the Hulk's defeat of an Asian tyrant, a bystander breathes a sigh of relief and mutters, "Safe at last!"

The Hulk growls, "Don't kid yourself! Nobody's safe!"

"What do you mean, Hulk?"

"I mean that you, and the rest of the weakling human race, will be safe when there ain't no more Hulk—and I'm plannin' on bein' around for a long, long time!"[5]

## Dueling the Inner Man

The contrast between Dr. Bruce Banner and his alter ego couldn't be starker. In the words of comic writer Stan Lee, "Where Dr. Banner had been gentle, the Hulk was a brute!

Where Banner had been civilized, the Hulk was a savage! Where Banner was a man, the Hulk was a monster!"[6]

During those times when the Hulk is submerged within Banner, the hapless scientist suffers the pangs of an anguished conscience. He surveys the destruction wrought by the Hulk and dreads the future. He especially fears that the Hulk will harm Betty Ross, the woman he loves, or Rick Jones, the teenager who knows the secret of Banner's dual identity and has befriended the doctor.

Banner is a well-meaning man, a believer in reason and logic, and he trusts his own ability to control the Hulk and eventually to cure himself. Nonetheless, every attempt to tame the Hulk fails. At first the Hulk only emerges after dark, and Banner devises a subterranean bunker in which he can lock himself before nightfall to be released by Rick Jones the next morning. This temporary measure doesn't last long before the Hulk smashes the reinforced door.

Soon additional exposure to gamma radiation strengthens the monster so that he emerges in the daylight. For a time, Rick Jones gains hypnotic command of the Hulk's behavior. But that calming influence is short-lived.

Banner devises a ray machine that turns him back and forth at will. Thanks to the machine, Banner's personality remains in control of the brute whenever the scientist transforms into the Hulk. Or so it seems to the well-meaning inventor.

The reader, however, realizes that Banner's control is slowly waning. Although Banner deceives himself into believing that he dominates the monster, the Hulk's speech patterns become more gruff and rude, less like Bruce Banner's cultured language. Likewise the behemoth's actions are increasingly vicious and violent, giving the lie to Banner's control. Not only does the Hulk's personality progressively overshadow Banner's, but with every transformation the monster grows more physically powerful, while the scientist becomes nearly invalid.

In issue #6, Banner's plight is demonstrated graphically. He attempts to turn himself into the Hulk in order to battle an invading menace, but the ray machine only works partially. In a grotesque twist, Banner becomes a composite creature with Banner's head and the Hulk's massive body. This frightening hybrid suggests that very little of Banner remains and the Hulk almost entirely controls their shared existence.

Most terrible of all for Bruce Banner is the dawning realization that the Hulk isn't a separate entity at all. The bestial Hulk represents the hidden dark side of Banner's own subconscious mind, the angry and aggressive persona Banner has always feared and repressed. Suddenly the habits and safeguards of a lifetime are inadequate. Morality, cooperation, acceptance, reason, compromise—all the bricks that build a civilized society—are shattered and scattered by the fury of the Hulk.

## The Heart of the Fury

Only many years later in the story of the Hulk do we learn the cause of Bruce Banner's inner anger. A violent and alcoholic father physically and emotionally victimized young Bruce. Too small and weak to strike back at his father, Banner swallowed his rage and resolved never to follow in the old man's footsteps. Unlike his abusive father, Bruce Banner devoted himself to self-control and personal discipline. He eschewed violence and committed himself to the path of dispassionate reason.

Banner's plan worked, or so it seemed. Unfortunately, anger and hate don't disappear just because we ignore them. Eventually Banner's long-denied feelings emerge with a vengeance—a gamma-powered vengeance. Tragically, the victim becomes the victimizer. The inner monster Bruce Banner kept tightly chained for so many years finally escapes and runs amok.

Readers hardly knew what to make of the angry, bitter Hulk. He wasn't fun or admirable. The only way to root for the Hulk was to pit him against a truly terrible foe, but the Hulk was no less monstrous after the other villain had been dispatched. Writer Stan Lee may have realized early on that he had dug himself into a pit with the Hulk. Perhaps to make the monster more palatable, the Hulk inexplicably changed colors between the first two issues. From dead-man gray the Hulk became emerald green, but a cosmetic change couldn't soften the underlying ugliness of the character. The original series lasted a mere six issues before being cancelled.

But even low sales couldn't destroy the indomitable Hulk. The creature made guest appearances for several years. In time, the Hulk got an ongoing strip in another comic; the Hulk took half the pages each month and another superhero got the other half. In a weird parallel of the Hulk's relationship with Bruce Banner, eventually the Hulk's strip squeezed out the other comic feature and took over the book entirely.

The Hulk has been published without interruption since then, and four decades have passed since his first appearance. Throughout that time the balance of control between Banner and the Hulk has seesawed back and forth, sometimes the man gaining the upper hand, then the monster ascendant again. In recent years Banner is usually at the mercy of the beast.

Not that we're surprised. The Hulk's gradual victory is exactly what we'd expect. After all, this comic book isn't really about a radiation-powered monster; it's actually about sin.

## Why the Hulk Always Wins

Doesn't this sound like something that might have escaped the lips of a guilt-tortured Bruce Banner?

> I do not understand what I do. For what I want to do I do not do, but what I hate I do. . . . For I have the desire to do what is good, but I cannot carry it out. For what I do is not the good I want to do; no, the evil I do not want to do—this I keep on doing. Now if I do what I do not want to do, it is no longer I who do it, but it is sin living in me that does it.

The words actually are from the apostle Paul's description of the power of sin in human life (Rom. 7:15, 18–20). Paul appears to write from bitter personal experience. Can you relate? At one time or another, hasn't each of us been perplexed and disgusted by our own actions? We swear we'll never again do a certain thing, then just a few weeks (or hours) later we find ourselves doing exactly that. Again. We are horrified by our own weakness, and resolve once more to be done with past behavior. But far too soon, we're back at it.

Why is it so hard to escape our own destructive patterns? Why do our carefully reasoned plans, our guilt-driven resolutions, and our this-time-for-sure vows prove so often inadequate?

In the terms of the superhero writers: The Hulk is stronger than we are.

In the terms of other comic strip writers, as the character Pogo would say, "We have met the enemy, and he is us."[7]

In terms I've used from the pulpit: When a sinner wrestles with himself, he cannot win.

Bruce Banner's miserable plight mirrors the experience of sinful humanity. Sin is a progressive disease. Sin never comes just this far and stops. The desert Bedouins have a cautionary saying: "If you let a camel put his nose in your tent on a chilly night, by morning the camel will be in the tent and you will be out in the cold." Sin is insatiable.

Bruce Banner's doomed efforts to master the Hulk remind us of our own futile strategies for quelling sin.

First Banner draws the line and determines the limits. The Hulk can emerge at night, but at no other time. The monster can come only this far. We allow sin a toehold and no more. As soon as sin crosses the line, we will stamp it out.

"I'll flirt a little, but that's as far as it goes," we tell ourselves.

"I'll stop after three drinks. I know when I've had enough."

"It can't hurt to listen to this gossip as long as I don't pass it on."

But soon the Hulk breaks the leash. The beast starts appearing in the daylight. The monster crosses the boundary, and regaining control is harder than we expected.

So Banner tries another tack. He can't control the Hulk, so he works out a compromise. After all, Banner has to live in the real world, and the Hulk is a reality. The Hulk can share Banner's existence, but only when expedient. When unavoidable, the Hulk can have his way.

We too make a treaty with sin and find handy excuses to justify our compromises.

"I don't like lying, but sometimes there's no other way to get by in this world."

"Why should I be the only one following the rules? I can't stay in business if I don't bend my scruples."

Whenever things get too tough, Banner frees the Hulk. The scientist forgets that he once got along quite well on his own. Strangely, the Hulk's presence becomes ever more essential. At some point compromise becomes the norm, and we exercise our principles just enough to maintain appearances. In a topsy-turvy reversal, the Hulk runs rampant and we restrain the brute only when absolutely necessary.

Finally a panicky Bruce Banner acknowledges his failure. The Hulk is gaining ground, so the hapless scientist looks for help from a new invention, a machine that will control the transformations. It's not so unlike the self-talk any one of us has engaged in on occasion.

"At last, here's the answer I've been looking for!"

"This pill will make everything all right."

"This self-help book will save me."

"This support group will be my life preserver."

Not that anyone should be embarrassed to seek assistance. Far from it. Asking for help is usually the wisest and healthiest option. It's the expectation that's often unrealistic—the pursuit of a quick fix, the search for someone else to take responsibility for our own wholeness, the hope for a gimmick that will save us while we continue self-destructive behavior.

Without a spiritual core, however, the props any of us leans on turn out to be broken crutches. We dare to hope things can be different. We make a little progress in the beginning. For a while, things get better. Then the Hulk rears his head. The gamma-ray machine fails us. The medication only masks our symptoms. The self-help regimen cracks and crumbles. The Hulk is free again and stronger than ever.

The Hulk is like sin, which is like an addiction that always demands a little more than last time. Haven't we all seen addiction at work? Haven't we seen decent people drink themselves to death, intelligent people eat themselves into the grave, and gamblers lose everything—family, home, job, savings, dignity—because they needed just one more win?

The reality is, humans can never make peace with the Hulk, because the Hulk will settle for nothing less than complete mastery.

"I tell you the truth," Jesus said, "everyone who sins is a slave to sin" (John 8:34).

## A Haunted Hero's Reward

In most of the Hulk's stories, he's seen railing at those around him, demanding to be left alone. Remember the haunting picture of the Hulk locked away in his underground bunker, pounding madly at the reinforced concrete walls? He is buried alive, utterly isolated from everyone and everything he cares about.

We see a flash of hope, then, when in one story the Hulk joins a superhero team called the Avengers, working beside other beings nearly as powerful as himself. The Hulk longs to find a family among these champions. But his membership in the Avengers lasts a mere two issues. After their second adventure together, the Hulk leaves the Avengers in a rage, assuring his partners that he doesn't need their companionship. The Hulk doesn't need anybody. To prove the point, he returns in the next issue to attack his former teammates.

In Peter David's tale *The Last Titan*, the Hulk gets his wish. He is left as the only intelligent creature on earth. A nuclear holocaust has destroyed every other human being, and the Hulk shares the ravaged planet only with swarms of cockroaches. Periodically the roaches attack the Hulk, devouring much of his flesh. The pain is excruciating, but the Hulk is so strong now that he heals within a few minutes.

As the Hulk and a decrepit Bruce Banner still share their existence, transforming back and forth, Banner wishes desperately to die. One night a heart attack grants his wish. At the exact moment Banner's life winks out, the Hulk emerges once more, this time for good. The story closes with the Hulk slumped on a desolate ledge, surveying the planet of which he is the sole ruler. At last he has overcome everyone. He has defeated puny Banner. Now he is left alone in an unending hell of isolation.

We should have seen it coming all along, right? Division. Unrest. Separation from everything and everyone worthwhile, even one's self. Isolation. Destruction and despair. After all, we've never seen the Hulk build or create. He's never the architect of something good. He simply smashes and destroys. He leaves wreckage and suffering in his wake.

As Bruce Banner discovered with the Hulk, sin separates us from ourselves. In a kind of internal wrestling match, as the apostle Paul described, sin turns us against ourselves, and we are caught between who we might have been and who we really are. Ultimately, sin extinguishes any kind of healthy self-love and replaces it with loathing; worst of all, sin separates us from our Creator—rebelling against God and building a wall between us. In the words of the Old Testament prophet, "your iniquities have separated you from your God; your sins have hidden his face from you" (Isa. 59:2).

Estrangement, loneliness, and the face of God hidden— these are descriptions of sin and of the Hulk's destiny: a living death. "For the wages of sin is death," the apostle Paul succinctly concludes (Rom. 6:23).

Long before Bruce Banner uttered similar words, Paul responded to this truth. "What a wretched man I am!" he said. "Who will rescue me from this body of death?" (Rom. 7:24).

That cry is so like Banner's that it echoes like a tragic Greek chorus as the Hulk roars, thumps his chest, and claims to be the mightiest one of all.

Yet, while the story of Bruce Banner and the Hulk may be symbolic of the human saga, it is not the whole story. The Hulk doesn't get the last word. For all Paul's gloomy assessment of the enslaving, destructive power of sin, he knows of a power stronger. There is One who is stronger and can free us from the Hulk, One who can save us from the monsters within ourselves.

Two other superheroes each claim to be that One. They can be convincing, too, that they are hero enough to tame the Hulk and help us get our lives back on track, for Batman and Iron Man seem invincible against great odds and carve believable paths to salvation.

# 3 Batman

# Guilt and Grace in Gotham City

The well-dressed couple and their son emerge from the movie theater and amble into the autumn evening. They stroll away from the marquee lights, treading on their own elongated shadows. The crowds thin and the streets darken as the Wayne family chats about the movie they have just seen, *The Mark of Zorro*. Young Bruce is particularly impressed by the adventures of the masked avenger. The boy strikes heroic poses with an imaginary sword and chatters on about the swashbuckling crusader, unaware that his own belief in justice is about to be tested in the crucible of suffering.

A hollow-eyed figure lunges from an unlit alley. The thug brandishes a gun and demands money. The moments that follow sear Bruce's memory forever, snapshots in a family album of horror.

A flash from the gun barrel.

His father toppling to the dirty pavement.

A second muzzle flare.

His mother's collapse.

The mugger fleeing.

A broken necklace scattering pearls into the gutter.

Bruce is the only survivor of the assault. Physically, the boy is unharmed, but all sense of order and reason bleeds from Bruce's life as he kneels beside his slain parents. At that moment Bruce makes a decision that will shape his future. He refuses to accept this violation. He will never allow this loss to heal. He will spend his life avenging this brutal atrocity.

And so Batman was born.

Eighteen years passed before Bruce Wayne donned the grim cowl and cape of Gotham City's protector. Nevertheless, his destiny was chiseled in granite the night Thomas and Martha Wayne died. In the ensuing eighteen years, Bruce organized the extensive family business to operate without his direct involvement. He honed his body with weight training, Olympic-level gymnastics, and martial arts. He mastered criminology, forensics, chemistry, engineering, computer science, and a dozen more fields. Drawing on the family fortune, Bruce Wayne built an arsenal of high-tech weapons and equipped his hidden headquarters in the huge cavern beneath Wayne Manor.

When Bruce deemed himself ready to undertake his mission, he donned a bizarre costume designed to terrify criminals. Inspired partly by his childhood hero Zorro but also by the fluttering bats in the cave beneath his estate, Bruce Wayne draped himself in a long cape and a cowl with bat ears. The uniform is black and gray, camouflage for a hunter of the night. Is it merely coincidental that black is also the hue of despair, the color of mourning?

Most superheroes put on a mask to hide their real identity. Not so with this caped vigilante. Bruce Wayne is the mask; Batman is the true identity. To devote himself wholly to fighting crime, Bruce Wayne forsook childhood, adolescence, romance, and normal human desires. The millionaire maintains just enough social life to divert suspicion from his nighttime crusade. As a result, Bruce Wayne is a two-dimensional prop, merely a façade behind which lurks the true person: the grim, driven, relentless Batman.

## Human Potential beyond Belief

Try to forget the corny Batman of the sixties television series, a campy character whose utility belt routinely produced collapsible ladders and shark repellant. Even forty years later, that SMASH-BANG-KAPOW parody remains an embarrassment to comic fans. As suggested by his origin story, the comic book Batman was a figure dark and fearsome. Sometimes meting out justice with a gun, he stalked the shadows in a never-ending quest to balance the scales for the murder of his parents. Perhaps pressured by parental watchdogs, comic book scripters soon had Batman abandon the gun and adopt a personal code against killing. Even so, this orphaned avenger remained dour and forbidding.

If possible, the comic stories of the last twenty-five years have created an even more severe Batman. Former Batman writer and editor Dennis O'Neil presents a disturbing picture of Bruce Wayne's alter ego. "The basic story is that [Batman] is an obsessed loner," O'Neil explains, "not crazy, not psychotic. There is a big difference between obsession and psychosis. Batman knows who he is and knows what drives him, and he chooses not to fight it. He permits his obsession to be the meaning of his life because he cannot think of anything better. He is also rife with natural gifts. He is possibly the only person in the world who could do what he is doing."[1]

Obsession and talent combine in Batman to create a character who demands our admiration and respect. In a world of superpowered heroes and villains, Batman excels through steely determination and uncompromising commitment. He does not fly. His skin will not repel bullets. He cannot see through walls or overturn cars or hurl blasts of energy from his fingertips. He is purely and simply human in every way, yet he routinely topples foes mightier than himself. Armed with cunning and scientific wonders, Batman has even bested Superman on occasion.

Batman is a founding member of the Justice League of America, an assembly of the most powerful heroes on earth. The membership list is a roll of titans: Superman, Wonder Woman, the Flash, and Green Lantern. Collectively these superhuman beings have power enough to move planets. One might expect an ordinary man in a cape to be cowed by such superhumans, yet Batman works beside them as an equal. In fact, when Batman temporarily departed from the League, the team was defeated and tottered on the brink of collapse. Although far greater in raw power, the other heroes depend upon Batman's tactical planning and indomitable spirit.

Behind the cowl, Batman is only a man, but he has made himself the absolute best that a man can be. Driving himself to the limits of human accomplishment, Batman has achieved the apex of physical and mental prowess. No one could work harder. No one could become more. Batman is the pinnacle of human potential.

He is also a failure.

Despite all his valiant efforts, Batman cannot save the world from violence and death. For every innocent victim Batman rescues from the grimy streets of Gotham City, the vices of poverty, drugs, and crime will slay a dozen more. Batman repeatedly defeats the Penguin, the Riddler, the Scarecrow, and the Mad Hatter, knowing full well that after a brief stay at Arkham Asylum, these fiends will inevitably escape to wreak more mayhem.

Sadly, Batman cannot even protect the few intimate friends he has allowed to enter his private world. In a truly horrific story in the late 1980s, the almost infallible Batman follows a false trail and unknowingly leaves his sidekick Robin to face the Joker alone in a warehouse. The Joker and his henchmen savagely beat Robin, and the Joker himself delivers the final blows with a crowbar. After Robin is broken and unconscious, the Joker departs, blowing up the building as he leaves.

Batman arrives mere minutes too late to save Robin. As he sifts through the smoking wreckage, he ponders his relationship with his young sidekick. He wonders why he took on a partner in the first place.

"I guess the truth is that I was lonely," he admits to himself. "Didn't want to go it alone. So what do I do? I bring a young innocent into this mad game."[2]

Batman's broodings end with the discovery of Robin's body. The hero's grief and guilt are palpable as he lifts the bloodied corpse in his arms. Appropriately, the storyline of Robin's murder was called "A Death in the Family."

Not long after Robin's death, the Joker again savages someone in Batman's inner circle. The Joker gains the upper hand in an encounter with Batgirl and guns her down. The heroine survives the attack but sustains incurable spinal injuries. Once athletic and acrobatic, Batgirl is permanently confined to a wheelchair. Fate's cruel lightning has struck again in Batman's life, and another innocent person has been laid low.

First Bruce Wayne watches his own parents die senselessly. Then he must accept the death of a young man whom he loved like a son. Finally he must come to terms with the crippling of a brave young woman whose only mistake is joining Batman's crusade. Three times Batman's loved ones have been attacked, and three times he has been powerless to rescue them.

We can forgive Batman for failing to protect every innocent and save every victim. He is, after all, only human. Unfortunately, Batman cannot forgive himself. His own heart tells him he should have tried harder. He should have done better. He should have been faster, stronger, smarter.

When Batman pursues the Joker after Robin's death, the villain's gunfire kills a luckless bystander.

"Another innocent sacrifice to the Joker's mania," Batman laments. "Another hapless victim to haunt my sleep."[3]

## Physician, Heal Thyself

In fact, the specter of guilt haunts Batman whether waking or sleeping. The true tragedy of the Dark Knight is not his failure to save the world but his inability to save himself. Behind the harsh mask of the ultimate crime fighter huddles a tearful little boy cradling the head of his dying mother. Batman passes through the world wrapped in mourning colors and guilt. His hard work and good deeds always fall short. He tries so fervently, but he never measures up in his own eyes. A lifetime of self-sacrifice and joyless virtue cannot atone for the guilt he carries. Even his muscled shoulders can scarcely bear that load.

Batman has much in common with the rich young man who asked Jesus how to find salvation (Matt. 19:16–26 NRSV).

"'Teacher, what good deed must I do to have eternal life?'" the man asked.

Jesus first reminded the young man that only God is good and we human beings should keep our "goodness" in proper perspective. Then Jesus pointed the seeker to the laws of Moses: "You shall not murder; You shall not

41

commit adultery; You shall not steal; You shall not bear false witness; Honor your father and mother; also, You shall love your neighbor as yourself."

Had the young man been older and wiser, Jesus's reply might have humbled him. After all, true law-keeping requires obedience that's inward as well as outward, and can anyone honestly claim to have never wished harm to another or harbored a lustful thought or stretched the truth?

But the young man was brash. "I have kept all these," he said. "What do I still lack?"

If we take his claims at face value, the wealthy young man must have been virtuous and upright. Here was a man trying hard to do the right thing and to live a good life from his childhood. He had memorized the law, crossed every inspired *t* and dotted every holy *i*. He kept every rule, gave alms to every beggar, prayed every day—and still it was not enough.

His question to Jesus exposed his doubts. If the young man were fully convinced of his own righteousness, why would he seek out the Nazarene teacher to ask about the requirements for eternal life? In spite of his zeal for the law, the young man worried that something was missing. The more scrupulously he kept the commandments, the more he feared falling short of God's requirements. He came looking for one more good deed to put him over the top, one more righteous act to silence the nagging doubts within his heart.

Where others might be tempted to write off such an arrogant fellow, Jesus saw something of promise and worth. Jesus answered, "If you wish to be perfect, go, sell your possessions, and give the money to the poor, and you will have treasure in heaven; then come, follow me."

Ouch. Jesus had put his finger on the issue: The young man wanted to be perfect, so unassailably good that the gates of heaven would fly open at his approach. Instead he found himself unready for the cost of perfection. He went away crestfallen because he couldn't bear to surrender his great wealth. He needed that money! How could he support his various charities, give alms to the poor, and bring his tithe to the temple without his fortune? How could Jesus expect him to give up his best tool in the search for perfect righteousness?

Afterwards Jesus told the disciples that it is easier for a camel to pass through the eye of a needle than for a rich man to enter God's kingdom. The disciples were shocked. If even the rich with their vast advantages cannot attain salvation, then how can anyone be saved?

Jesus looked at them and said, "For mortals it is impossible, but for God all things are possible."

What was Jesus saying? That wealth is an evil force?

Hardly. Money is not evil. The evil resides in misplaced priorities. Wealth tempts us to trust our own resources. As long as we believe we can provide for ourselves, by ourselves, we have no reason to put our faith in God. Jesus didn't require all his followers to give up their money. Perhaps he made this demand of the rich young man precisely to show that the seeker had never admitted the limits of his own obedience, nor was he willing to place his full trust in God. Instead he had spent a lifetime trusting himself. He trusted his wealth. He trusted his position in the community, his own virtue and good deeds. But he never learned how to trust God. So he wandered away sadly to work still harder, keep more rules, and pile up even more good works.

Jesus was painfully clear. If we can save ourselves, we do not need God. If we cannot save ourselves, then we need God above all else. We cannot have it both ways. We must accept one alternative or the other. We must either place our whole faith in God or, like Batman, rely upon ourselves—our wealth, goodness, dedication, hard work, and self-sacrifice.

43

## Company in the Bat Cave

In every place I've ever worked (and these days I work in a church), I find people trying so very hard to make themselves okay, and in many cases better than okay—good, exemplary. These folks will always take on one more job, serve on one more committee, write one more check.

Batman would fit right in. In fact, church would be a good place for Batman to hang out and always find a warm welcome. Who isn't delighted with the hard-working colleague, the good-deed-doing neighbor, the dedicated, self-sacrificing servant to the church? But are the good deeds, determination, best intentions, and sacrifices so selfless?

The apostle Paul wouldn't think so. For years Paul was a driven man, obsessed with rule-keeping, good-deed-doing, and salvation-seeking. He eagerly and diligently persecuted anyone who went against the rules of Jewish law.

One day Paul's obsession with doing "right" was confronted by Jesus. Grace *calls* us to serve and guilt *drives* us to serve, Jesus showed Paul. Though these two forces may look all the same on the outside, there is a big difference inside between being called and feeling driven. It's the difference between working hard because you're feeling saved, thankful, and so filled with excitement that you just can't sit still or keep quiet, and slaving away because you feel lost and scared, driven and desperate.

Jesus lovingly offered an escape from the dead end of salvation by works, and Paul took it. The rich young man, however, found the offer just too much. Did he think the offer too expensive, requiring him to hand over forever his greatest superpower—wealth? Or did he fear the offer was one more sham, just too good to be true? In any case, the rich man could not surrender his search for salvation

44

through personal goodness. In spite of his doubts, he clung to his desperate quest for self-justification.

Batman is caught in precisely the same tragic quandary. The shadowy crime fighter is a noble but heartbreaking figure. Betrayed by the apparent random cruelty of life, Batman lacks faith in anything or anyone beyond himself. He operates on a simple philosophy: "The world only makes sense," he says, "when you force it to."[4] He relies entirely on his own strength, intellect, and determination. In spite of losses that would have broken many people, Batman fights on.

In *Batman: The Dark Knight Returns*, considered by many to be the ultimate Batman story, writer and artist Frank Miller depicts an aging Batman's continuing pursuit of salvation. At an undesignated time in the future, Batman has retired from crime fighting. In the ten years since he gave up the cape and cowl, Bruce Wayne has grown morose. He broods and numbs himself with alcohol. Since Batman disappeared, Gotham City has become a cesspool of viciousness and mindless violence.

In a key scene, Bruce Wayne sits alone late at night staring through a window. He wrestles with the temptation to bring Batman out of retirement. Miller's artwork is simple but evocative. One panel shows a portion of the window, the mullions forming a stark cross. Next we see a bat flying outside the window, juxtaposed to the cross. Miller then shows us the shadow of the cross falling across Bruce Wayne's troubled face. These images repeat with increasing intensity until the bat crashes through the window in a cascade of glass shards and broken mullions.[5]

In that moment Bruce Wayne's decision is made, and he once again dons the costume of the Batman. The Dark Knight cannot accept the way of the cross; he returns to the way of the bat and sets out once more to save himself by his own heroic efforts. Initially he revels in his decision, caught up in euphoria. As he leaps into action against the backdrop of the city, he muses, "The rain on my chest is a baptism. I'm born again."[6]

But Batman's rebirth and salvation are only a temporary illusion. His own sense of unworthiness emerges again within a few pages. While disarming a bomb, Batman thinks, "If I had the time or the right, I'd say a prayer."[7]

In an even more telling moment, the supposedly born again Batman stares into the eyes of Two-Face, a villain psychologically scarred by shame and self-hatred.

"Take a look," says Two-Face, flaunting his own ugliness. Staring intently, Batman replies, "I see a reflection."[8]

Is this the sound of a man with a new life?

It sounds more like the voice of a man longing for salvation and still falling short—the sound of a man whose vocabulary is missing the word "surrender."

The truth is, Batman's sole hope for peace and redemption lies precisely in surrendering himself to forgiveness. Only when Batman gives up the quest for personal perfection will he be able to welcome the grace that cannot be earned. Although Batman is as good as any human being could be, he will never be good enough. Neither hard work nor good works can free Bruce Wayne from the guilt and despair that torment him; no matter how fiercely he tries, Batman can never save himself. No one can. With human beings, this is impossible.

Or is it?

If muscle and mind fall short, maybe microchips and steel can save us. Where we can't save ourselves, perhaps technology can do it for us. Science never lets us down. Science always finds a way. Science is our hope for the future. At least this is the creed of the armored avenger Iron Man.

Peek behind Iron Man's metal mask and see if he's right.

# 4

# Salvation
# by Success

**T**ony Stark had it all—a magazine cover life of glamour, achievement, and riches. He was a brilliant inventor and technician with a bright future; his present was nothing to sneeze at either. Only in his twenties, Stark was already a wealthy man, thanks to his weapons research and munitions manufacturing plants. Blessed with rugged good looks and a natural flair for the high life, Tony was the paparazzi's darling, as he frequented the elite clubs with a different beautiful starlet or supermodel draped on his arm every night. Life offered Tony nothing less than the best of everything.

Then one day everything changed. Tony Stark's heart got broken. Literally.

To encourage confidence in his latest weapons technology, Stark agreed to supervise the field testing of his new micro-transistorized armaments. But this testing wasn't a simulation exercise. Stark's weapons were deployed in the jungle battlefields of Vietnam, and the inventor himself went along to see his creations in action. He should have stayed home.

At first, everything went perfectly. The new high-tech weapons functioned flawlessly, and American soldiers routed the Vietcong. In the aftermath of the one-sided battle, Stark strolled through the jungle with an army officer, savoring the victory. Then the millionaire scientist stumbled over an unseen trip wire. The ensuing explosion killed the handful of American soldiers who accompanied Stark.

Tony Stark himself survived, but just barely. The explosion had riddled his body with shrapnel. When the Vietcong found Stark's unconscious form, his civilian clothing convinced the enemy that the wounded man might be an American dignitary, perhaps a politician. They carried the bleeding inventor to their commander Wong Chu. An examination of Stark's identification papers revealed his occupation, and an examination of his wounds revealed he had only a few weeks to live. The explosion had injured Stark's heart. Even worse, shrapnel was embedded in his chest, slowly working its way toward the heart. The shrapnel was too close to the heart to remove by surgery. The injury was a ticking time bomb, and Tony Stark's days were on a countdown.

Wong Chu decided to milk the opportunity fate had placed in his hands. He told Tony Stark about his internal injuries—with one significant lie added. Wong Chu claimed that his doctors could save Stark's life. If Stark would develop a weapon for Wong Chu's personal use, then the Vietcong commander would order the life-saving surgery.

Tony Stark pretended to cooperate with Wong Chu. He knew his heart was beyond the help of surgery, but Stark was also a man to make the most of his opportunities. Turned loose in a warehouse of machinery, tools, and scrap iron, Stark determined to build a weapon he could use to bring down Wong Chu, even if it were his final action in the land of the living.

Fearing that Stark might die before the weapon was completed, Wong Chu gave the American inventor an assistant, an aged Chinese scientist named Yinsen. The old man had long been a prisoner of the Communists, and at first he refused to cooperate with Stark. Only when Tony revealed his plan to turn the weapon against their captors did Yinsen enthusiastically join the project.

The machine Tony Stark envisioned was simultaneously an engine of destruction and a lifesaver. Feverishly he and Yinsen crafted a massive suit of mechanized body armor. The iron suit would be impregnable to conventional weapons. Built into the suit were various offensive weapons, but most important for Stark was the heart-supporting circuitry wired into the chest plate. If all went according to plan, Tony Stark's new weapon would assure his own survival as well as the downfall of his captor.

As the work proceeded, Stark's cardiac pains became more frequent and more severe. At times he was almost incapacitated, and Yinsen pushed ahead with the work in a desperate race against death. In the end, they had no time to test the armor. As the final work was completed, Tony Stark collapsed and Yinsen frantically fitted the battle suit onto the dying inventor. Just as Yinsen put the last piece of mechanized armor in place, a jerry-rigged alarm warned the scientists that Wong Chu was on his way to the lab. Even though the armor was completed, charging the suit to full operational power would require several minutes.

During the energizing process, Stark was helpless and the armor was little more than an iron cage. To gain time, Yinsen tried to lure Wong Chu away from the laboratory where Tony Stark lay immobilized. The elderly scientist ran into the corridor shouting threats at the Vietcong warlord. Wong Chu was not to be deterred; at his order, guards contemptuously gunned down the unarmed Yinsen.

Tony Stark heard the grim events unfold outside the lab. Somehow, he vowed, he would find vengeance for his friend Yinsen.

When Wong Chu broke into the lab, neither Stark nor the promised weapon could be found. Wong Chu was enraged and mounted a search for the missing scientist. Little did the warlord realize that he had only to raise his eyes to find the armored inventor. Stark hid in the shadows of the laboratory ceiling using powerful transistorized suction devices.

With each passing minute, the armor became more fully charged, and Tony Stark mastered the basics of movement within his new, mechanized body. He unleashed his vengeance in hand-to-hand combat so humbling that the frightened Wong Chu dubbed his foe an ironclad avenger. "Iron Man" was born.

Unfortunately, the armor temporarily exhausted its internal power, and while the suit was recharging, Wong Chu fled from Stark. In an act of sheer vindictiveness, the warlord determined to kill all his prisoners before Iron Man could stop him.

Unable to pursue Wong Chu, Stark hatched a last-ditch plan. He expelled some of the armor's oil supply in a pressurized stream, squirting the oil past the sprinting Wong Chu and splashing it against an ammunition storage shed. Igniting the trail of oil, Stark exploded the ammunition reserves just as Wong Chu drew abreast of the shed. The warlord was caught in the full force of the conflagration.

Yinsen's murder was avenged. Iron Man had won the first of many victories.

## Stronger, Faster, . . . Better?

In its original incarnation the prototype armor was clunky and artistically drab, resembling a wrought iron deep-sea diving suit. In the second issue, Tony Stark tried to counter the grim demeanor of his armored identity by painting his suit golden yellow. The brighter tint helped a little, but the bulky body armor still evoked the impression of a painfully clumsy dreadnought. The helmet was a nearly expressionless lump of iron in the shape of a watermelon. The arms and legs were cylindrical and stocky, the fingers like blunt sausages.

Nor was the armor's built-in weaponry particularly impressive. The cover blurb for Iron Man's first appearance in *Tales of Suspense* #39 declared, "He lives! He walks! He conquers!"

Aside from a few gimmicks, initially the armor didn't do much beyond walking. In his first adventure, Iron Man deployed compressed air jets from his boots, suction cups, a miniature transmitter, a magnet, a finger saw, and a cigarette lighter. Nice gadgets, but hardly a heavyweight arsenal in the fight against evil.

The armor evolved dramatically over the next few months. New weapons appeared. The unsettling tendency for the armor to lose power came far less frequently. Ten issues after his debut, Tony Stark designed an entirely new battle suit. In *Tales of Suspense* #48, the "new" Iron Man burst upon the scene. His armor was positively svelte compared to the original suit. "Flexible" metal alloy revealed the muscular contours of Tony Stark's arms and legs. His breastplate, gauntlets, and boots were more compact and more powerful. The face mask was expressive, and the entire armor was rendered in red and gold. For the first time, Iron Man actually looked like a superhero instead of a radio-controlled automaton.

In the forty years since his origin, Iron Man's armor has gone through countless innovations and improvements— stronger and lighter alloys, better power sources, and an ever-increasing battery of weapons. With each reincarnation, Iron Man created specialized battle suits for stealth missions, undersea exploits, and outer space battles. One armored outfit actually had chameleon abilities, changing color to match the background of the terrain.

The improvements in Iron Man's armor are a visual parable, one that insists technology will inevitably improve. Science has no limits. Each scientific breakthrough is merely a prelude for the next great leap forward. If we can't invent something to fix your problems today, just stick around; we'll figure out how to do it tomorrow.

If anything, Tony Stark's story shows that the same technology that might have ended his life also transformed him into a superhero. Maybe he did have it all (wealth, romance, intelligence, accomplishment, and good looks) as Tony Stark, inventor. But doesn't he have more as Iron Man, literally wrapped in cutting-edge technology?

## Man of Metal in Hope of a Heart

Like anyone, Tony Stark has longed for certainty and safety. He's believed hard work, brains, and determination can build a good future. Relying on his own cleverness and determination, he's built the weapons company he inherited from his father into a multi-billion-dollar corporation. In fact, he's built several such companies.

He's had to. When the top-secret U.S. espionage agency SHIELD decided that Stark International's withdrawal from weapons production posed a potential threat to United States security, a quiet buyout proceeded. SHIELD acquired fifty-one percent of the stock in Stark International, and though Stark was eventually able to reclaim control from SHIELD, it was to no avail. He later lost the company entirely in a hostile takeover mounted by unethical business rival Obadiah Stane.

Stark then built a new company from scratch and dubbed it Stark Enterprises. But after Stark's apparent death, his cousin inherited the company and sold it. Tony Stark "returned from the dead" but decided not to go to court to reclaim Stark Enterprises. Instead, once more relying on his inner resources, he moved on to found Stark Solutions.

Clearly, Tony Stark is a genius at building successful companies. Just as clearly, he's not very good at holding on to them.

If wealth were to be the fortress Stark would build round himself, it would be made of walls continually needing to be propped up and reinforced. Even when the money flowed freely, Stark was too busy, too embattled, and at least occasionally too embittered to appreciate the advantages his money could buy.

What about romance? Surely that particular wall stands firm in the house that Stark built. True, Stark's dated scores of beautiful women; a revolving-door procession of gorgeous socialites always seems in wait for him. But problems abound. For many years he's had to protect his injured heart and double identity as Iron Man by wearing an iron chest plate that must remain a secret from even his closest friends. That means he can never lower his guard with the women he dates. Even a casual hug might give away his secret; this is not the stuff of which love or even intimacy is made.

In fact, the first great love of Tony Stark's life was his administrative assistant Pepper Potts. For years Tony loved Pepper in silence, afraid to entrust her with his most cherished secret; Pepper was also in love with Tony. But Stark waited too long to confess his feelings, the moment passed, and Pepper married Tony's employee and friend, "Happy" Hogan.

Even after Tony Stark found a way to free himself from the iron chest plate that kept him alive, his romantic life

53

remained a saga of disappointment and disillusionment. Perhaps the story of Stark's love life is summed up by his relationship with Kathleen Dare: This former love interest nearly killed him by shooting him and leaving him paralyzed for months.

You might think Stark could ease his loneliness with a glittering social life of fashionable clubs, box seats for opening night, jaunts to the Riviera, and the finest fare that money can buy. Surely this alone is enough to make life worthwhile. But beneath the peeling gilt paint, this wall of Stark's fortress is also cracked and crumbling. Exhausted from building empires, lovelorn and lonely, he too often looks for comfort and courage in the bottle. Some of the hardest trials in his troubled life have been made immeasurably worse by his addiction to alcohol. What began as social recreation turns into a deadly disease.

Stark's dead-end existence is like what I once found behind a door in a church I'd visited. The church had two doors behind the pulpit area, one on each side of the front wall. The resident minister told me one door led to a little room used for hanging robes and storing worship supplies. And the other? Take a look, the minister invited, smiling. I opened the second door and found myself facing a blank brick wall. The minister explained that the architect had installed that second door merely to balance the first and "improve the appearance" of the room.

This has been Tony Stark's experience. Neither wealth nor romance has brought the struggling hero any abiding joy. In spite of promises of pleasure and living the high life, he's opened a promising door that's led nowhere. He's found only addiction, self-loathing, and emptiness. He's smashed painfully into a brick wall. The fortress he's built to provide for his own salvation has teetered; every potential savior has either failed or betrayed him.

54

Yet one wall remains—one that just might be strong enough to hold the whole house together—the wall built from the bricks and mortar of science and technology.

Technology, after all, has been the one thing in life on which Tony Stark has always been able to rely. Technology made him rich, kept his injured heart beating, transformed a playboy into a superhero, and offered Iron Man salvation.

## Blessing or Curse?

Years after becoming Iron Man, Tony Stark discovers that many of his scientific secrets have been stolen by one Justin Hammer, who in turn has brokered that technology to a host of supervillains. Stark contemplates with horror the list of science-enhanced criminals using his know-how to prey upon innocent people. Ultimately, he anguishes, he is responsible for every theft, extortion, and murder committed with his inventions.

As soon as possible, Iron Man tracks down the villains he's inadvertently empowered. In every case he recovers or permanently disables his pirated technology. Along the way, however, he accidentally causes two deaths. This raises the toll of victims for whom Stark feels responsible and further fuels the fires of his personal guilt.

Even worse, when the American government becomes aware of the deaths caused by Iron Man, the authorities mistakenly assume that the ironclad hero is dangerously out of control. To stop Iron Man's apparent rampage, a covert government agency unleashes its own monstrously mechanized operative code-named Firepower.

In a dramatic showdown, Firepower outguns the beleaguered Iron Man, who must fake his own death in order to escape. Ironically, Firepower's vast weaponry is also

55

based on Tony Stark's stolen designs. Of course, Iron Man does later defeat Firepower, but the story hints that the inventor's own runaway technology may eventually bring about his downfall.

Other storylines raise the same warning. In one, a robotic Life Model Decoy created by SHIELD usurps the armor, and Tony Stark squares off against his own battle suit in hostile hands.

In another story, Iron Man's armor shuts down and its circuits fuse following a slugfest with the Hulk. Tony Stark is trapped inside the immobilized armor, without oxygen, while his friends race the clock to release him from the nearly impregnable battle suit. Iron Man's temporary imprisonment within his own invention mirrors the larger situation of Tony Stark's growing dependency upon the armor.

The natural question becomes a nagging one: Is Tony Stark complete without his mechanical crutch?

Indeed, the Iron Man shell sometimes seems more real than the man inside the armor. On several occasions other people have donned Iron Man's armor. James Rhodes, "Happy" Hogan, Clayton Wilson, and even a woman, Bethany Cabe, have all "become" Iron Man at various times, and the world never noticed the difference. Unlike most superheroes, in Iron Man's case the clothes really do make the man. The armor is essential, but Tony Stark seems almost expendable.

The situation becomes more poignant and more sinister when in one story the battle suit defies its own creator and repeatedly sabotages Stark's efforts. As he spies on enemies in a darkened room, the armor's chest lamp inexplicably lights up, revealing Iron Man's presence. While on an undersea mission, the sealing plates in Iron Man's face mask open, threatening to drown him before he can reach the surface. Later, while flying over New York City, one of his jet boots misfires, sending Iron Man careening in a headlong dive. In the culminating moment of betrayal, Iron Man is greeting a foreign ambassador when the repulsor ray in his gauntlet apparently fires of its own accord. The ambassador dies instantly in the blast while the world watches on television. Iron Man is branded a murderer.

Avid readers will know that Justin Hammer has found a way to control Iron Man's armor from afar, triggering these "malfunctions." Even so, the implications are clear: The armor is mightier than the man within, and in a battle between Iron Man and Tony Stark, the machine is certain to destroy the human.

Eventually this very scenario plays out. Due to the convergence of several freakish circumstances including a direct lightning strike, Iron Man's armor actually becomes self-aware. As the suit takes on a life of its own, it is at first eager to please its master, but soon the Frankenstein story is played out with twenty-first-century trappings. The armor cold-bloodedly murders a man, and Stark is helpless to stop it. Appalled by its creator's "weakness," the armor turns against its inventor.

Stark inventively dons an earlier suit of armor to fight his sentient armor, but the battle is one-sided. The living armor pounds its creator and rages about Stark's betrayal in wearing a different battle suit, ripping away the inferior battle suit piece by piece, screaming, "You're mine, Tony! Mine! MINE!"[1]

This chilling moment reveals that the machine has become the master with the man as the servant. Tony Stark is now the possession of his own handiwork.

In a final to-the-death confrontation on a deserted island, the armor removes its mask to reveal a mechanical face beneath. The renegade machine has begun to build a body within the armor. With a little latex skin, the living armor can soon play the roles of both Iron Man and Tony Stark. The invention is prepared to utterly usurp the inventor. Soon Tony Stark, the man, will be irrelevant and outdated.

Stark does finally prevail over the living armor in a victory both haunting and ironic. During the desperate battle, he suffers a heart attack. As he collapses before his own creation, Tony Stark challenges the machine to finish him off so that at least he can die like a man. The armor repeats the words, "Die like a man," then rams an iron fist into its own chest cavity and yanks out a tentacled metal heart. With its dying strength the sputtering armor attaches the mechanical heart to Tony Stark's chest. As the inventor revives, the armor whispers again, "Die like a man." Having asserted its own heroism and humanity, the smoking armor collapses in death after saving the life of its creator.[2]

The unsettling resolution of the story disturbs us. We'd been rooting for Tony Stark, of course, but the living armor's sacrifice leaves us wondering who is the real hero. More to the point, Stark was beaten at every turn by the machine, and in the end the machine even outmatches Stark in nobility. In a final bitter reversal, the machine that was given life by Stark now returns the favor. Stark's own weakness is underlined by the fact that he survives due entirely to the mechanical heart grafted to his chest.

The armor might do quite well on its own, but Tony Stark has no life apart from his invention. Far from being a savior for Tony Stark, technology has become both his master and his nemesis.

So much for the house that Tony Stark built. Although surgery can eventually repair Stark and remove the life-threatening shrapnel, in the profoundest sense the hero still plods through life with a broken heart, one which all the science and wealth in the world cannot heal.

## Iron Will, Rusted Life

At least one biblical hero would empathize with Iron Man's plight. Like Tony Stark, the Old Testament's David had it all: good looks, women, heroism, fame, wealth, and the kingship of Israel.

Mind you, David had to work for it. Remember the story of the shepherd boy squaring off against Goliath? The Philistine giant not only topped David by several feet, but he was armed with the ultimate technology of his day—iron. Goliath's armor was bronze, but the iron head of his spear weighed in at fifteen pounds; presumably his sword was also made of iron. The Philistines knew the secret of working iron, but the Israelites didn't. One reason the Israelites were so hard pressed by the Philistines was because Philistine iron inevitably prevailed against Israelite bronze.

King Saul wanted to give David a little help against Goliath, so Saul ordered that David be dressed in the king's own armor. But Saul's war gear was too large and heavy for David, more a liability than an asset. Besides, David knew that armor and technology would not decide the outcome of his confrontation with the giant. The battle would favor the one who trusted God. Sure enough, armed only with a sling and five smooth stones, David vanquished Goliath, and in an unexpected upset the shepherd boy used Goliath's own fearsome iron sword to behead the fallen giant.

This was David at his best, relying entirely upon God. Sadly, David did not always practice such wisdom. As he grew in power and prestige, David increasingly relied upon himself and his own resources. For a while that strategy appeared to work.

The Israelites learned the secret of working iron, and David's iron-bladed forces ended the Philistine threat once and for all.

When David had a spat with his wife Michal, he simply put her away and broke off relations. After all, he had other wives and concubines.

When his heart lusted for the married Bathsheba, David pulled some strings and had her soldier husband killed in battle.

When you can take everything you want, why deny yourself anything? When your own hand can fulfill your heart's desire, why call on God?

Yes, David had it all . . . until he stopped relying on God. When David began to put his faith in iron—the iron of his sword, the iron of his troops, the iron of his own will—everything turned to rust.

Maybe you've never heard this part of the story: David's family fell apart. One son died in infancy as a result of David's infidelity. Another son, Amnon, actually raped his half-sister Tamar. Yet another son, Absalom, later murdered Amnon in revenge. Inexplicably, David did nothing to address these issues. Perhaps he was crippled by the memories of his own indiscretions and violent deeds.

David's kingdom also tottered. Years after killing Amnon, Absalom raised a revolt against David and sent his father fleeing into the wilderness. David's closest adviser sided with Absalom and joined the revolt. In the battle that regained the throne for David, the bloodthirsty Joab slew Absalom. In doing so, Joab expressly disobeyed David's orders to spare his son. Absalom's death broke the aging king's heart.

In his last years, David's wives plotted behind his back, each vying to put her own son on the throne. On his deathbed, David spent his last breath planning revenge on his enemies, coaching his heir Solomon on whom to kill as soon as he claimed the throne. Joab was at the top of the list. And within a generation of David's death, the kingdom he had built by blood and iron was divided by civil war, never to be reunited.

## The Heart of the Matter

When everything is added up, David's life was sad and lonely. The shepherd-king had it all, then lost it all: wealth, power, romance, the technology of iron. The house that David built ended up looking a lot like the house that Tony Stark would build three thousand years later.

Even so, David had his moments of clarity and insight. While he did not always act on this wisdom, David knew that reliance on traditional battle armor was a vain hope.

"The LORD is my strength and my shield," David asserts (Ps. 28:7), recognizing that spiritual armor provides more ultimate protection than the latest defense technology. In the New Testament, the apostle Paul builds on this idea and urges the Ephesian Christians to put on the armor that will protect them from head to toe, armor made of truth, righteousness, faith, and salvation (Eph. 6:10–17).

Scarcely anyone would willingly reject the benefits available to us in the modern world: inoculations, life-saving medical procedures, health insurance, retirement plans, and automobiles engineered for our protection. Used wisely, these are gifts from God for which we can be deeply grateful.

Yet these measures can no more guarantee our security than Iron Man's armor can insure his well-being. Money, technology, and success are the exalted trinity of our achievement-driven culture, but these false gods cannot save us. How else can we explain the sad fact that our scientific progress is outstripped only by our rising dependence upon antidepressants?

In Psalm 51 David ponders how success has failed to bring him happiness and peace. As Israel's king reflects upon his own failings, he confesses his deepest need. What David craves is not more wives, more iron, or more power. David already has all the outward gifts the world can give. What he yearns for is an inward gift, a healing transformation within himself. "Create in me a clean heart, O God," David prays, "and put a new and right spirit within me" (Ps. 51:10 NRSV).

In utter honesty, David admits that his problems have very little to do with what goes on around him. That's why riches, royalty, and iron can't soothe David's misery. What goes on inside of David is the source of his troubles. Like Tony Stark, David's crisis is essentially a heart problem. He aches for a purity he cannot achieve on his own, a spirit right with God. In the words of a later prophet, David needs a new heart, a living heart transplanted to replace a heart of stone (Ezek. 36:26).

In Iron Man's darkest night of the soul—struggling with addiction, watching his corporation being stolen by rivals, battling his own rebel technology—Tony Stark has probably raised a cry similar to that of David in Psalm 51. Perhaps you have done so as well in your own dark times. Few of us can claim to never have leaned upon an empty hope or placed faith in a false salvation. Most of us discover by bitter experience the chinks in our own armor and the limits of worldly security. Such experiences can break us, but they may also point us in a new direction.

As I write these words, Tony Stark's fortunes are rebounding. His new romance is admittedly rocky but might still be salvaged. He has cleared himself of spurious accusations. Recent injuries are healing, and Stark is reconnecting with alienated friends. Perhaps things are finally turning around for the ironclad avenger.

However, I suspect that Iron Man will soon find himself mired in some new personal crisis. Part of this is the nature of an ongoing monthly narrative; a painless life makes a boring story. But even beyond the demands of good storytelling, something seems fundamentally awry in Tony Stark's life. For all his considerable gifts, he remains strangely unfulfilled. As he searches for personal salvation through riches, romance, pleasure, and technology, could he be looking for the right thing in the wrong places?

Iron Man keeps placing his faith in externals, but his most persistent problems arise from within. Behind the armor, Tony Stark remains as insecure and vulnerable as ever. Maybe he has overlooked a crucial clue in his own origin.

Remember that moment in the crude laboratory in Vietnam when Tony Stark reclined helplessly on a table, wrapped in the work of his own hands? He lay there with his life on the line, waiting for the battle suit to charge itself with life-saving energy, as outside in the hallway the Chinese scientist Yinsen selflessly laid down his own life so Tony Stark could have a second chance. Does Iron Man remember that he owes his life not to a high-tech battle suit but to a sacrificial death offered up on his behalf?

Life from death.

Salvation from sacrifice.

Deliverance unearned and freely given.

Tony Stark has bravely walked one dead-end road after another, but he has yet to find the path that leads to a new beginning and a joy that doesn't fail. No wonder. It's an unlikely road, and a particularly unappealing path for those who insist on trusting their own accomplishments.

It takes a real superhero to know his greatest work can be done on the day his strength runs out.

# Superman Revisited

# Death, Resurrection, and Doomsday

**H**e was the first superhero, and nearly seven decades later he remains probably the greatest. In sheer power, few heroes approach him. In nobility, no comic book character surpasses him. Because of his goodness, cynics sometimes call him the Boy Scout, though he considers the nickname more a badge of honor than an insult.

You've already been introduced, of course, to Superman, the Man of Steel, who has a glorious record of catching falling airliners, propping up collapsing bridges, diverting floods, and evacuating whole villages from the path of flowing lava. He's rescued innocent people from house fires, tornadoes, tidal waves, wild animals, and rampaging criminals; practiced random acts of kindness on a truly global scale; and made a positive difference in countless lives.

Yet Superman's illustrious career has left the world fundamentally unchanged and humanity profoundly unreformed. What's the problem? If the man from Krypton combines rare goodness with matchless strength, why hasn't he saved the world? He has the power we lack, so why doesn't he feed the hungry? He is strong enough to disarm any nation, so why doesn't he end war? He has access to Kryptonian technology and alien science in his Fortress of Solitude, so why doesn't he cure cancer, clean up pollution, and halt the environmental degradation of the planet? Why doesn't Superman end racial prejudice, ethnic genocide, and social exploitation?

Because he can't. The job is too big for even Superman.

## Drat These Failing Superpowers!

Writer Paul Dini and artist Alex Ross poignantly explore Superman's possibilities and limits in an oversized comic called *Superman: Peace on Earth*. As Superman ponders the problem of world hunger, he recalls his childhood on a Kansas farm. Clark Kent's adoptive father taught him that the earth provides enough for everyone. The problem, according to Pa Kent, is that people don't take care of one another. Individuals get so caught up in personal agendas that they fail to watch over their neighbors.

Convicted by these early teachings and inspired by the Christmas season, Superman decides he will try to make a lasting difference in the world. He will feed as many people as he can, and in the process he will set an example of compassion and assistance.

The Man of Steel addresses the U.S. Congress and asks permission to distribute America's surplus food to the needy people of the world. With some trepidation, Congress agrees. Unharvested fields, stockpiles set to spoil, and surpluses will be gathered, and Superman will use that food to feed as many people as he can in a single day. While Superman prepares for his massive undertaking, a

66

bemused world looks on. Some are skeptica
in to help, volunteering to gather and load
   On the designated day, Superman begir
deliver loaded trucks, full freight cars, ar
beds piled high with grain and staples. H
American reservation in the western United States. He
carries food to a Brazilian barrio. He touches down in
Africa, Asia, and Europe.

   Superman feels good about his effort, but he worries
that a one-day blitz is far too little to make a genuine
difference. In one war-torn country, a small boy asks if
Superman will be back with more food tomorrow. Superman has no answer for the child. At another locale, starv-
ing people riot and fight for their share of the food. In yet
another place, fearful crowds pelt Superman with stones,
suspicious of his motives. One nation's smiling dictator
welcomes Superman, intending to seize the food for his
own profit. Superman does his best to see that the food is
distributed to the needy, but once he flies away, he cannot
know for certain that supplies will reach the people for
whom they're intended.

   As the long day draws to a close, Superman carries
a shipload of precious food to a nation whose government has forbidden his visit. The people of the land are
in desperate need, but the government wishes to retain
complete sovereignty over the populace, and Superman's
act of goodwill is unwelcome.

   Ignoring government orders, Superman enters the nation's airspace hoping to deliver the food quickly and depart
before a confrontation develops. He has misjudged, though,
the determination of the totalitarian rulers. While the Man
of Steel is still high overhead, a missile launches skyward.
Burdened with a ship full of grain, Superman cannot dodge
the rocket. The ship explodes, spilling charred grain to the

arth. Worse yet, the missile carried a payload of chemical toxins. The grain that survives the explosion is poisoned.

Superman lands to survey the wreckage. He kneels among piles of smoldering, contaminated wheat. He thinks of those who refused his gift today. He laments the many hungry people whom he did not reach in his global effort. He worries about those who will be hungry again as soon as this food is eaten. Superman bows his head in despair and admits to himself that his grand gesture has failed.

Superman can rescue only so many people.

## Frantic Heroism

In the series *Astro City*, Kurt Busiek has created the superhero Samaritan as an apparent homage to Superman. Samaritan is constantly monitoring the world situation and dashing off to avert impending disaster or to combat super-powered villains. In one amusing story from *Astro City* #6, Samaritan attempts to cultivate a social life.

Dressed in civilian clothes, Samaritan tries to have a normal dinner date with his friend and sometime superhero partner Winged Victory. But, predictably, Samaritan is continually distracted. He appears to maintain polite chitchat, but his mind is elsewhere as his super senses register a never-ending stream of cataclysm and catastrophe. After dinner the couple allow themselves a single brief kiss, then each flies in a different direction to deal with emergencies. Both Samaritan and Winged Victory seem relieved to shed the pretense of a social life and get back to work.

Plainly there is always one more victim to rescue, one more threat to face, one more villain to subdue. The diligent superhero will never catch up, much less get ahead. Anyone who is willing and able could try to rescue the world 24-7 and never meet all the needs. Saving the world requires something more than selfless, frantic heroism by a superhuman few.

Superman acknowledges this following his disappointing mission to feed the world. In a statement to the media, he invites others to follow his example in their own way and at their own level. He admits that world hunger will be abolished not through superhuman effort but only through a concerted human effort. When people in every walk of life become committed to helping one another, the world will change. When ordinary people pool their energies and resources to build just governments and compassionate economies, a new day will begin.

You see, Superman knows he can snuff out forest fires, but how can he prevent the carelessness and indifference that often begin those fires? Superman might be able to come up with a cure for cancer, but wouldn't we cause new cancers with the chemicals we concoct to use for pesticides, sweeteners, and preservatives? Perhaps Superman could find a way to stretch our fossil fuels, but what could he do about the selfish spirit that takes more than it needs? Even if Superman did banish violence from our schools, how would he cure the causes of violence rooted in poverty, despair, and domestic abuse? The man from Krypton knows: He may be superhuman, but he is still human. He might be able to stop certain kinds of behavior, but even Superman cannot change the human heart.

Ultimately, we need to be saved from ourselves.

## Death Becomes Us

If Superman really wants to save the world, he's faced, realistically, with two alternatives: either force humanity to behave or spend his life minimizing the harm we do to one another.

In *Kingdom Come*, a grim vision of a possible future, writer Mark Waid shows us both choices carried to the extreme. In Gotham City, an aging Batman has decided to enforce his notions of right behavior. Batman's robots and drones police the city around the clock. Criminal activities are quickly detected and dealt with severely. Law and order prevail, but Gotham City has become a fascist state, and ordinary citizens look over their shoulders in fear. No one dares cross the line established by Batman.

In the same storyline, the Flash has assumed a different mantle in nearby Keystone City—not the enforcer but the protector. Moving too fast to be seen or heard, the Flash tirelessly crisscrosses the city and guards its citizens from every accident, mishap, and crime. Automobile crashes are averted, explosions smothered, and falling ladders righted. The city is safe, but this never-resting rescue mission of the Flash is both lonely and frighteningly obsessive.

Refusing to rule the world, even for a noble purpose, Superman chooses to be a rescuer too. Although he fulfills the role exceptionally well, a scene from the 1978 film *Superman: The Movie*, starring Christopher Reeve, reveals the limits of that role: Lois Lane has been killed, but a heartbroken Superman refuses to accept her death. Taking flight, Superman circles the globe in the opposite direction of Earth's rotation. As Superman flies ever faster, the Earth slows down and finally reverses its spin. This causes time to move backward and allows Superman to undo the events that led to Lois Lane's death.

Despite the far-fetched plot device—a time-reversing gimmick that would never "fly" in a contemporary Superman comic book—Superman comes through for Lois. The Metropolis Marvel overcomes the ultimate foe and plucks his love from the gaping grave. Superman has saved Lois Lane from death.

Right?

Not really.

Superman has rescued Lois once again, but strictly speaking he hasn't saved her from death. Lois is still doomed to die like every other mortal. Superman has only postponed her demise. Sooner or later Lois Lane will make an unwilling address change from Metropolis to necropolis. Maybe she will slip in the shower. Perhaps she will die in a helicopter crash while covering a big story. With luck, she will pass away in her sleep the day after her one hundredth birthday. Whatever the particulars, Lois has an unbreakable appointment with Mr. G. Reaper.

The fact of death reminds us what we human beings can and cannot do for one another.

## Emergency versus Eternity

In common speech the terms *save* and *rescue* may be used interchangeably, but don't they mean different things?

"Rescue" certainly describes the important work of both superheroes and real heroes like firefighters, police officers, EMTs, surgeons, and relief workers, who routinely give people more years of life.

To "save," though, is different—bigger, more lasting. Where rescuing postpones death and preserves life, saving overcomes death and transforms life. Rescue is temporary; salvation is eternal.

Superman, alas, is a rescuer, not a savior. He can soar between worlds, divert the course of rivers, listen to the dance of molecules, squeeze anthracite into diamonds with one hand, stare granite into magma, and rescue whole cities from destruction. But he cannot save a single life or transform the human heart. Against the reality and finality of death, Superman is as helpless as anyone else and eventually will die like everyone else.

In fact, Superman did die in 1993. His downfall arrived in the form of Doomsday, an inhuman figure of terrible destruction. Doomsday wasn't seeking money, power, or conquest; he simply wanted to eradicate every living thing. Doomsday was the laboratory creation of Bertron, an alien genetic scientist working to create a being that could survive in any environment. The alien geneticist did indeed engineer a creature able to regenerate itself after dying. In the process of returning to life, the creature evolved invulnerability to the force that killed it. As Bertron subjected Doomsday to thousands of horrible deaths, Doomsday became stronger with each regeneration, but the angry memory of every death imprinted itself upon the creature's primitive mind.

Eventually the now-invincible Doomsday kills Bertron and breaks loose upon an unprepared and fragile world. Doomsday perceives even the most harmless living creature as a potential threat to his existence. He begins to cut a swath of destruction, murdering every animal or human within his reach.

Along with Superman, the other superheroes take their turn against Doomsday. Living legends such as Green Lantern and the Martian Manhunter fall like October leaves. Doomsday scatters and humbles them all. After several bouts, only Superman has the strength to resume the fight, and by now Doomsday is marching toward Metropolis. Superman's city is on the line and millions of lives are at stake, including those of his closest friends and his beloved Lois.

Superman goes to battle alone; it's long and brutal. Superman is unaccustomed to the taste of blood and the stabbing anguish of broken bones. At one point a cry for help rouses him from unconsciousness. Wobbling in flight, Superman offers his help to rescue children from a burning orphanage. The bruised and bloodied Superman is in far worse condition than the children evacuated from the flames. He briefly accepts an oxygen mask, but as soon as his head clears, he forces his protesting body back into the fray.

By now, Doomsday is in downtown Metropolis. Fallen buildings and smoldering cars litter the streets. Soldiers and police are utterly ineffectual. When Superman arrives to make his last stand, Metropolis looks as if World War III has struck.

The final battle is illustrated in equally dramatic terms—full-page panels in *Superman* #75, where Doomsday is more fearsome than ever. Throughout the battle he has continued to evolve defenses. Bony spikes now bristle from his fists. His leathery skin extrudes dagger-sharp spurs at every joint. He shows no sign of fatigue or weakness; Superman, on the other hand, is half-dead. Bruises cover his swollen face. His proud uniform is tattered, and open wounds spill Kryptonian blood in the street. While rescuing a falling news copter, Superman gives Lois Lane a last kiss. Then he plunges back into battle, vowing to fight to the end.

The end comes soon. The titans pound each other with such fearsome strikes that windows shatter from the concussive blast. The force explodes a crater beneath their feet. The briefest lull ensues while Superman and Doomsday gather strength for the final assault. Their blows land simultaneously. The battle ends in tragic, costly victory.

The city is saved. Doomsday is dead. His conqueror lies sprawled beside him. Lois Lane hurls herself forward to embrace the fading Superman. She begs him to hang on

73

until the paramedics arrive. Almost unconscious, Superman is oblivious to his own wounds. His concern is for the people of Metropolis and the world.

"Doomsday . . . ," he gasps. "Is he . . . Is he . . ."

"You stopped him!" Lois assures him. "You saved us all!"[1]

## Picture Salvation

In 1993, DC Comics sold a special bagged version of *Superman* #75 containing a poster and a *Daily Planet* newspaper clipping that reported the death of Superman. The bagged edition also included a black armband emblazoned with the Superman insignia. These symbols of grief may seem silly in retrospect, but not at the time.

Newspapers and television networks gave Superman's shuffle from this mortal coil plenty of coverage. Evening news stories recounted Superman's demise for weeks, and even people who didn't regularly read comics suddenly made a run to the shops for more of the story. DC Comics was caught off guard by the swell of public interest; in response, the writers lengthened the story arc and delayed Superman's return for some months . . . because, of course, Superman *would* come back. Superheroes nearly always come back, and comic fans couldn't imagine a world without Superman.

At the time, though, after reading *Superman* #75, we felt that something unthinkable had happened. Death had claimed someone too good to die. A symbol had passed away.

Indeed, one finds it difficult not to read symbolism into Superman's death. Consider the enemy Superman dies to defeat. Doomsday is a typically heavy-handed comic book name for a villain. In this case, however, the name scarcely

74

exaggerates the creature's potential for devastation. The whole world is at risk unless some champion can stop this dreadnought. We are not surprised that the comic book writers borrow biblical language to describe Doomsday as the "Armageddon creature."

Consider this scene too: As Superman flies away from the burning orphanage, one of the rescued children asks what kind of monster Superman is fighting. A caregiver answers, "From the way he's behavin', I'd say he's the devil incarnate . . . usherin' in the end of the world."[2]

Truly Doomsday is as close to the personification of wickedness as comic books can evoke. Theologically, he represents more-than-human evil, intent on destroying God's good creation. However, the monster's name carries an additional message we might easily overlook. In Old English the meaning of *doom* was "judgment." To face doom was to stand under judgment for one's deeds. In its original sense, *doomsday* was a religious phrase denoting the last judgment of God at the end of time. No wonder *doom* came to mean "death"—doesn't the thought of trying to defend our lives in the presence of God frighten the best of us? In any fair trial before God, we fear we are doomed indeed. In this sense, the monstrous Doomsday also represents the judgment that condemns us in our own eyes.

Facing an evil of this magnitude, Superman could not simply beat Doomsday into submission or jail him for his crimes. Doomsday was too powerful for an easy victory—he combined death, evil, and judgment into one terrifying figure. In retrospect, the stakes were too high for a cheap win. The defeat of this gigantic threat demanded a heavy price.

Superman had taken it upon himself to be humanity's champion, and the one who came from above had to finally lay down his life to fulfill his mission. No lesser effort would have halted the onslaught of evil. No smaller sacrifice would ransom those in the path of destruction.

You can know Superman is a fictional character and still be moved by his story. His death brought tears to my own eyes and echoed a much older story, this one true. Behind the slumped figure of the dead Superman, an upright piece of broken lumber juts from the wreckage. The tattered cape of the Man of Steel hangs on the board and flutters in the wind. In my eyes, that heaven-reaching timber casts the shadow of the cross over the scene. Superman is no savior, but his dying to rescue Metropolis points our hearts toward the true Savior who died for the world.

We are up against a power greater than ourselves. Call it Doomsday, sin, evil, or Satan, but you must admit we are outmatched. On our own, we cannot defeat this enemy because, in truth, some inward part of us collaborates with this force. Our good deeds and our hard work will never be enough to claim victory—just ask Batman. Wealth, success, and technology will not redeem us, either; Iron Man is proof enough of that. The powers of this world will fail us in the heat of battle; rescuers may come to our aid, but even the noblest and strongest of them cannot truly save us.

For us to escape the fate that stalks us, someone must die in our place. Some hero must interpose himself and accept the killing blow meant for us. Then he must rise again to love us for all eternity. He must embrace us with a love that transforms our hearts, saves us from ourselves, and teaches us to love in return.

Where can we find a hero so worthy?

The cover of *Superman* #75 is tombstone gray bearing these chiseled words: HERE LIES EARTH'S GREATEST HERO.

With all due respect to Superman, I know a greater hero who is more than a rescuer.

Read the inscription in the black-and-white of the New Testament: "There is salvation in no one else, for there is no other name under heaven given among mortals by which we must be saved" (Acts 4:12 NRSV).

Jesus is now and forever our Savior. At the cost of his own life, Jesus conquered sin, death, and doomsday on our behalf. To put it simply, Jesus went to hell and back to save his own. Even death could not hold him, and he lives today, renewing—not just rescuing—life for all who love him.

This is no ancient fable or venerable myth. This is the truest story of all; every other tale about good overcoming evil merely echoes this Great Story from the center of time and the heart of God.

In the poignant closing page of Superman's death tale, a weeping Lois Lane holds the bloody, lifeless figure of Superman in her arms. The pose evokes the well-known sculpture of Mary cradling the crucified body of Jesus. The homage to Michelangelo is unnecessary, however. The comparison is inevitable. Never before or since has Superman appeared so divine. For all of Superman's powers, all his good deeds and mighty victories, it's this moment of brokenness when he truly appears like Christ. In the past, Superman rescued countless people, but on this day he laid down his life for his people.

Isn't this what salvation looks like?

# 6  Wonder Woman
## The Power of Truth

**E**ver since her debut in 1941, Wonder Woman has been an oddity in the world of superheroes. She's entered "a man's world" to seek peaceful solutions for conflicts driven by violence and power fantasies. She's brought to the comic book universe of powerful males and helpless women a character both heroic and unapologetically feminine. In a market where characters rise and fall like shooting stars, the Amazon princess has not only survived but has become an icon who stands proudly alongside Superman and Batman.

What sets Wonder Woman apart from her peers?

Could it be that where other heroes are driven by a quest for revenge, justice, or retribution, Wonder Woman has found her purpose in two more abstract pillars—the liberating powers of freedom and truth?

Or is it that at a time when most comic book characters were created by youthful writers and artists with minimal education, Wonder Woman was the brainchild of a Harvard-educated psychologist and lawyer?

The answer lies with both the motivations given Wonder Woman and the creator who designed her to begin with.

# To Tell the Truth

If intellectuals and scientists are expected to be stodgy bookworms sequestered in classrooms and laboratories, William Moulton Marston broke the mold. With a knack for marketing himself and getting his ideas into the public eye, Marston, the creator of Wonder Woman, became a minor celebrity in the thirties and forties. He wrote both popular and scholarly books, served as an adviser to movie studios, and penned national magazine columns. Most of his projects related in one way or another to his groundbreaking work on the lie detector and his constant search for truth.

Marston, you see, is generally considered to be the inventor of the modern lie detector. While still studying at Harvard, he created a crude device that detected deception based on his idea that lying creates a physical tension revealed in the rise of blood pressure. (Later versions of the lie detector would also measure levels of perspiration and changes in respiration.)

Nowadays lie detectors are often disputed as unreliable, but Marston garnered considerable renown for his invention. Along with defending his ideas in scholarly journals, Marston courted the popular media. During World War I he tested accused spies; arranged publicity stunts using the polygraph to determine the personality types of blondes, brunettes, and redheads (photo spreads in *Look* magazine popularized Marston's lie detector for romantic matchmaking); and even used the polygraph to compare the comfort levels of men using different brands of razor blades!

Psychology is the science in which we seek the truth about ourselves, and the field of deception detection genuinely fascinated Marston. His belief in the power of truth would influence his creation of Wonder Woman, as would other beliefs. At least philosophically, Marston was a pacifist who hoped humanity would find nonviolent ways of settling our differences. He was also a freethinker when it came to the role of women. He predicted that within a few decades America would evolve into a society ruled by women. Far from being threatened by such a change, Marston was convinced that the world would be a better and safer place thanks to the growing feminine influence.

Looking for a way to promote his ideas and to provide a positive role model for young girls, Marston turned his eye to the new and rapidly growing industry of superhero comics. He was ever eager to position himself favorably and was soon appointed to the editorial advisory board of the All-American and DC comic lines. At that point Marston was in the right place to pitch his idea for a new kind of superhero. Writing under the pen name of Charles Moulton, he published the first Wonder Woman story as a back-up feature in *All Star Comics* #8. One month later, Wonder Woman became the cover feature in the newly launched *Sensation Comics*.

Her origin story was a heady mixture of superhero adventure, Greek mythology, romance, feminism, pacifism, and wartime patriotism. On a hidden island dwelled a race of Amazons who had withdrawn from the male-dominated world. When American fighter pilot Steve Trevor crashed on the island, the Amazons reluctantly took him in and tended his injuries. The Amazon Queen Hippolyte decided that when Trevor returned to the outside world, an Amazon should accompany him. This ambassador would carry the values of Paradise Island into "man's world" to promote freedom and democracy. After a rigorous competition, Hippolyte's daughter Diana was chosen to wear the mantle of Wonder Woman.

Along with her abilities as an Amazon native, Wonder Woman left Paradise Island armed with unique weapons. On each wrist she wore the large bracelets adopted by all Amazons. The bracelets recalled a time when the Amazons had been enslaved and chained by a tribe of brutal men led by Hercules—and they remained on many Amazons' wrists as a continuing reminder of servitude long after their escape to Paradise Island. This wristwear figures prominently in "bullets and bracelets," a recurring game in which Wonder Woman deflects bullets fired at her by bouncing them off her bracelets.

Complementing the bracelets is Wonder Woman's hallmark weapon: her magic, golden lasso, known in contemporary stories as her Lasso of Truth. Along with the many predictable uses of an unbreakable lariat, the lasso compelled obedience from anyone wrapped in its coils. In theory Wonder Woman could require a rope-bound prisoner to obey any command, but in practice the lariat was typically used to compel the captive to speak the truth. No captive could lie to Wonder Woman while encircled by the magic lasso.

Over time the notion of obedience waned and discerning the truth became the primary use of the magic lariat; as Wonder Woman evolved, the lasso became more important. In fact, it is central to the meaning of her character: Wonder Woman is guided by the truth revealed through the golden lasso. At the same time, she's the guardian of that truth.

Represented by the golden lasso, truth is Wonder Woman's primary weapon in the war against evil.

## Truth as a Weapon

Sure, Wonder Woman is good at deflecting bullets with the flick of a wrist, but in a story from *Sensation Comics*

#28, a criminal uses a more deadly weapon: invisible gas. Attacked and stunned by a criminal's gas gun, Wonder Woman wakes up bound and lying on a railroad track. The gas has left her confused and uncertain of her identity. She convinces herself that she's tied up with her own unbreakable magic lasso. Even though a train is approaching, the Amazon ceases to struggle. Her fate is sealed by her belief that escape is impossible.

Fortunately, Wonder Woman's mother is aware of her danger and contacts her telepathically. She reminds her daughter of her true identity and assures her that she is tied up with an ordinary rope. Realizing the truth of her situation, Wonder Woman easily breaks her bonds and halts the oncoming train.

Marston was criticized for too frequently tying, chaining, and binding Wonder Woman. He even introduced the idea that if a man could weld Wonder Woman's bracelets together, she would lose all her Amazon powers. Repetitious or not, the theme of being bound is a strong symbol of enslavement to falsehood. Lies bind us and make us helpless. In the face of such lies, truth is the best weapon in our arsenal. Wonder Woman frees herself from the train tracks only after she sees the truth.

Real life teaches precisely the same lesson. Phoebe was an active member of her church, an above average college student, and a dutiful daughter. No one else knew that the young woman was also anorexic. She disguised her eating disorder with the pretense of already having eaten or being under the weather or practicing the typically awful dietary habits of college kids. Phoebe even deceived herself as she maintained the illusion that "keeping her weight down" was healthy.

Phoebe's parents finally saw and confronted their daughter's illness. Forced to face the reality of her self-destructive behavior, Phoebe entered counseling and got involved in a group devoted to overcoming eating disorders. Along the way she also began to confront at least some of the inner demons that originally led to her anorexia. When we talked about her health, she told me that part of getting well was learning to accept herself.

"For the first time in my life," Phoebe said, "I'm figuring out who I really am. Not who I pretend to be. Not what other people want me to be. I'm learning how to be the real me. If that's not good enough for everybody else, I'm sorry, but it's just who I am."

Truth is a valuable weapon in dealing with disorders like anorexia—or maybe "tool" is a better word than "weapon." Understanding ourselves and facing the truth of our sickness is almost always the first step in getting well, whether from anorexia, addiction, anger, fear, marital problems, cancer, heart disease, or nearly any other illness of body, spirit, or family. "You will know the truth," says Jesus, "and the truth will set you free" (John 8:32).

Lies wrap us in a web of captivity, each strand strengthening our imprisonment. Have you ever noticed that the lies we tell others tend to multiply? One lie leads to another and another. As we scramble to maintain our deceptions, we weave an increasingly complicated tapestry of lies.

A man confessed to me that he was actually relieved when his wife found out he'd been cheating on her. "The lies were killing me," he said. "The adultery itself was a kind of lie, and then I had to keep telling more lies to cover it up. My whole life had become a lie. Even getting caught was better than living like that."

If the lies we tell others are destructive, the lies we tell ourselves are even worse. Whether it's Wonder Woman deceiving herself that she had no way to escape the approaching train or the college woman rehearsing the lie that her abnormal eating habits are actually healthy, the end result is a bondage that destroys us. Truth is the only cure.

## The Shape of Truth

Many people in our contemporary culture assume that truth is subjective and situational. In other words, whatever I happen to believe is true for me, and whatever you choose to believe is true for you. In that way of thinking, truth is soft clay we can shape to suit our particular preferences. No absolute standards exist; everyone makes up his or her own truth.

This view of reality is impossible to defend. Mimicking something he'd seen on television, a young friend of mine leaped from a second story window using a trash bag as a parachute. He wholeheartedly believed that the black plastic bag would float him gently to earth. The broken collarbone he suffered a few seconds later contradicted this belief. Gravity turned out to be true regardless of his opinions on the matter.

Certainly everyone should be free to choose his or her own beliefs and opinions. However, the insistence that truth is whatever you make it leads us into a nightmarish swamp where nothing is certain or solid. If every opinion carries equal weight and every philosophy is equally valid, then truth is nothing more than the flavor of the month. If the only truth is my own beliefs, then I will never find a truth bigger than myself. To put it bluntly, truth can set us free, but opinions cannot. On the contrary, our false beliefs and self-deceptions are the very chains from which we must be liberated.

In the storyline collected in *JLA: Golden Perfect*, Wonder Woman's Lasso of Truth is broken in battle. As a result, truth itself breaks down in the world. Instead of objective

84

truth ruling the universe, whatever people believe becomes fact. Two plus one equals four. Subatomic particles misbehave. The sun revolves around the earth, and the moon turns to green cheese. The earth becomes flat. Reality literally unravels, and the world is saved just in time by the repair of the Lasso of Truth.

The story is a powerful parable about the nature of the world. Truth is not shaped by opinion or consensus. Truth is what it is regardless of whether we believe it. Many people today think that the truth is shaped by our beliefs. Just the opposite is the case. Our beliefs must be shaped by the truth, or else we are fooling ourselves. When we accept the truth, we are set free to see life as it really is; when we reject the truth, we enslave ourselves to lies and falsehood.

Jesus once told a parable about two men who went to the temple to get right with God. One man was a tax collector. The Jewish people hated tax collectors because they made themselves rich by charging exorbitant dues and also collaborated with the Roman rulers. This tax collector was so disgusted by his own sinful life that he dared not even raise his eyes toward heaven. Sobbing and pounding his chest, he repeated one heartbroken prayer over and over: "God, be merciful to me, a sinner!"

The other man was a Pharisee, one of the super-righteous religious professionals of that day. The Pharisees were famous for their extreme keeping of every tiny detail of religious law and ritual. The Pharisee stood tall and proud before God. In his prayer he congratulated himself on his habits of fasting and tithing. "God, I thank you that I am not like other people: thieves, rogues, adulterers, or even like this tax collector" (see Luke 18:9–14 NRSV).

Who do you suppose left the temple set right with God?

The tax collector, of course. The Pharisee remained wrapped up in the lie of his own perfection. Unable to admit his need for forgiveness, the Pharisee didn't bother to ask for forgiveness. The tax collector, on the other hand, saw the truth about himself and asked for God's mercy.

An early promotional cartoon shows a smiling Wonder Woman gleefully shattering heavy chains bearing labels like PREJUDICE and MAN'S SUPERIORITY. That cartoon explained Wonder Woman's purpose in the world, but it could just as easily describe the ministry of Jesus, who said, "So if the Son sets you free, you will be free indeed" (John 8:36).

Jesus sets us free by showing us the truth. Jesus himself describes his mission in this way: "For this reason I was born, and for this I came into the world, to testify to the truth" (John 18:37).

Another crucial question confronts us at this point: Which truth does Jesus have in mind? The truth Jesus offers us is like a coin with two faces. On the one hand, Jesus unveils the truth about who we are. On the other hand, Jesus also opens our eyes to the truth about who we can become if we have eyes to see and ears to hear. Jesus reveals the whole truth about ourselves, both the selves we are and the selves God calls us to be.

## Makeover Madness

Knowing ourselves is not as easy as it sounds, not even for the wielder of the Lasso of Truth. In fact, if anyone has the right to a full-fledged identity crisis, it's Wonder Woman! She's been redefined again and again by different writers and artists as an Amazonian princess, a warrior, a peacemaker, a superhero, an ambassador, a goddess, and even Mrs. Superman.

During Robert Kanigher's term as writer during the fifties and sixties, Wonder Woman succumbed to feminine stereotypes in silly stories about alien suitors, marriage fantasies, and letters from the lovelorn. In the early seventies Diana underwent another radical makeover, abandoning both her uniform and her powers to become a mod-styled, karate-chopping secret agent. At about the same time, Gloria Steinem seized on an earlier version of Wonder Woman as a larger-than-life symbol of feminism, making her the cover feature in the very first issue of *Ms.* magazine.

Will the real Wonder Woman please stand up? Poor Diana has had too many voices telling her what to do.

We've all had the same experience. Well-meaning people tell us who we ought to be. Conflicting desires confuse us. Circumstances pull us in different directions. One of the great challenges of life is discovering our true selves.

My favorite Wonder Woman story is a graphic novel written and painted by Christopher Moeller. In *JLA: A League of One*, we discover that Diana practices the discipline of regular self-examination. Periodically Wonder Woman retires to the privacy of her home island and drapes the coils of the magic rope around her own neck.

"Show me that which my heart conceals," she says to the Lasso of Truth. "Loose thy pure and perfect light. Let thy servant stand revealed."[1]

Within the revealing light of truth, Wonder Woman searches her being for any self-deception or falsehood. She reviews her life for any missteps that may have taken her from the path of truth. The process is arduous and exhausting, even for an Amazon princess. How many of us have the courage to face our true selves without blinders or delusions?

Who am I? Who are you? The question is not what we pretend to be, nor what we want to be, nor even what others judge us to be, but who we are when the light of truth dispels all the shadowy illusions.

## Remembering Earthen Roots

In Wonder Woman's very first story, she's established as the daughter of the Amazons' Queen Hippolyte. Perhaps you're wondering how a daughter could be born to the queen of an exclusively female society. The answer lies in the peculiar mythology of Paradise Island. Queen Hippolyte fashioned a baby girl from clay, and the Greek gods gave life to the earthen sculpture—Diana, who grew up to be Wonder Woman.

More than once, Wonder Woman's enemies have literally turned her back into clay, forcibly reminding the princess of her humble beginnings. In every circumstance, challenge, and calling, Diana would do well to remember she is a creature of clay given the blessing of life by powers higher than her own.

Perhaps you and I would also benefit from that particular insight. Behind the trappings of Greek mythology, the story of Wonder Woman's "birth" calls to mind the account of humanity's creation in the second chapter of Genesis: "the LORD God formed man from the dust of the ground and breathed into his nostrils the breath of life, and man became a living being" (Gen. 2:7).

Like Wonder Woman, we too are created from clay. The name of our first father Adam derives from a Hebrew word that means "ground" or "earth." Even our English words "human" and "humble" descend from *humus*, the Latin word for soil. Driving past a cemetery reminds us of our humble human stature. We came from the earth, and when our days are spent we will return to the earth.

This is the truth about who we are. We are living clay. We did not make ourselves. We are not God; we are human beings. We are not the Creator; we are merely God's creatures. Unless we grasp this truth, we will inevitably live our lives either in fear or in rebellion.

Knowing that we are God's handiwork liberates us from so many lies and falsehoods. Accepting that we are created beings frees us from the terrible burden of playing God. We aren't self-sufficient, and we don't have to be. God gave us life, and God will provide what we need for fullness of life.

Being creatures means we are not expected to save ourselves by our own hard work and goodness. God made us, God loves us, and God will never abandon us. God freely gives salvation to all who seek it from his hand.

Living within our limits frees us from taking responsibility for the actions of others and allows us to be gentle with ourselves when we fall short of what others expect from us. Our neighbors are answerable to the Creator for their own lives. So are we. Although we owe love and support to one another, ultimately God alone can show us who we are meant to be. Whether we satisfy the expectations of parents, teachers, preachers, bosses, and spouses is irrelevant.

Accepting our humanity reassures us that we don't have to guess at the meaning of life or make up our own role in the world. The meaning of life is God's job (a job God is perfectly able to handle without our help), and our calling is simply to live in a humble and loving relationship with our Creator.

Ah, but there's the rub! Part of the bitter truth we must accept is our ongoing failure to love and trust God. We creatures of clay have fallen short of God's hopes for us. Sometimes we excuse our mistakes by saying, "I'm only human," but being human is not our problem. On the contrary, most troubles arise because we reject our humanity. We keep trying to be something else. We refuse to live within God-given boundaries. We pretend we can save ourselves. We prop up our sagging self-esteem by lording it over others.

We sprint toward a dead end when we deny our need for God and try to become complete apart from God. God made us, and God knows our "specs." Why do we deceive ourselves that we know more about life than God does? God is in the best position to help us understand ourselves, including both our boundaries and our potential. When we reject God's guidelines, we close our eyes to the truth and become entangled by lies.

This has been our problem since the Garden of Eden, when the serpent convinced Eve that her personal fulfillment lay in disobeying God. That lie of self-sufficiency still haunts us to this day. Every sin we commit is a lie, a deception that contradicts our true nature and our rightful relationship with God.

To make matters worse, we deny that anything is wrong. We don't need any help, thank you very much, because we don't have a problem. *Sin* is such a harsh word. We're not sinners. We're just . . . righteousness-challenged.

As Robin might have said on the old television show, "Holy self-deception, Batman!"

## Bound by Something Higher

"What is truth?" asked a cynical Pontius Pilate when Jesus was on trial (John 18:38).

Jesus didn't reply to the mocking Roman because Jesus had already answered the question: "I am the way and the truth and the life" (John 14:6).

Now there's a bold declaration! Many people through history have offered to teach us the truth, but Jesus claims to be the truth. In himself, Jesus claims, he reveals the greatness and abundance of a life lived in faithful dependence upon God. He reminds us that we cannot build such lives on our own as he extends the helping hand of God to all those who acknowledge their need for it. When we see the truth clearly in Jesus, we understand both our need and God's provision.

In the New Testament John insists, "If we claim to be without sin, we deceive ourselves and the truth is not in us" (1 John 1:8). As long as we refuse to accept the full truth about ourselves, we are like the person who avoids the doctor's office for fear of hearing bad news. Avoidance and pretense will not save us from cancer or sin. The bad news of facing our illness is the necessary prelude for the good news of getting well.

Think of this another way: The finest precision-performance automobile filled with the highest-octane gasoline is incomplete in itself. That car lacks life or purpose until a driver turns the key and sets his hand on the steering wheel. Then the journey begins and the possibilities are endless. Cars don't drive on their own, and people don't live on their own. We are going nowhere until we yield to God. We are incomplete until we welcome God's presence.

William Moulton Marston died of lung cancer in 1947. Shortly before, in what was probably the last story he wrote for Wonder Woman, Marston put these words into the mouth of Queen Hippolyte: "The only real happiness for anybody is to be found in obedience to loving authority."[2]

That's as much wisdom as we'll discover in the coils of the golden lasso. In the arms of Christ we can learn the rest: The only real happiness for anybody is to be found in obedience to God's loving authority.

And that's the truth.

# 7 Thor

## Transformation

**A** frail man kneels on the earth and strikes his walking stick upon the ground. In a blinding flash the unimpressive figure disappears, replaced by the steel-muscled Thor, the master of lightning and the hammer-wielding prince of Asgard. The metamorphosis of Don Blake into the mighty Thor was one of the most dramatic and familiar scenes in comicdom during the Marvel renaissance of the 1960s. Younger readers might have assumed Thor was a new twist on the superhero myth, but actually he was the latest heir of a long lineage.

Transformation is the stock-in-trade of comic book creators. Metamorphosis puts bread on the table for superhero writers, and that's been the case since the beginning of the superhero business. Just think of rumpled Clark Kent ducking into that handy phone booth to emerge an instant later as the indomitable Superman.

In 1940 the transformation gimmick was distilled to its purest form when Billy Batson first shouted, "Shazam!" and was instantly transmogrified into the scarlet-garbed do-gooder Captain Marvel. The good Captain may not have been the first transforming hero, but he exemplifies the theme: weakness converted into power, lowliness elevated to greatness—and all in the blink of an eye.

Billy Batson was an orphaned newsboy. Lured into an abandoned subway station, he met a wizened Egyptian magician who gave him the magic word *Shazam*, a mystical acronym that bestowed the gifts of the ancients: Solomon's wisdom, Hercules's strength, Atlas's stamina, Zeus's power, Achilles's courage, and Mercury's speed.

At the mere utterance of "Shazam," a flash of lightning turned Billy Batson into the invincible Captain Marvel. The tongue-in-cheek Captain flew, crashed through walls, hoisted automobiles, and repeatedly thwarted the evil plans of the insidious Dr. Sivana. When the danger was past and the adventure ended, once again saying "Shazam" reversed the change and restored Billy Batson to his true identity. Billy would return to his mundane daily round, but in his heart he carried the glowing secret of his greater identity, and the magic word lingered on the tip of his tongue.

Through the 1940s Fawcett Comics, the publishers of *Captain Marvel*, defended themselves against a lawsuit alleging that their character infringed on DC Comics' copyrighted Superman. By 1953 DC finally succeeded where Dr. Sivana had failed: Fawcett Comics brought Captain Marvel to an end.

However, the cat was already out of the bag. Future new superheroes might bear less resemblance to Superman, but the transformed-into-a-wonderful-new-identity-in-a-flash kind was here to stay. This was stuff to fire the imagination. Who could escape a chill when, amidst mysterious swirls of mist, Jack Ryder converted to the maniacal and contorted Creeper? What red-blooded boy wouldn't feel a pang of envy when Congo Bill transferred his mind into the powerful body of Congorilla? Who didn't long to be

93

Rick Jones when he clashed his wristbands to swap places with an alien hero from the Negative Zone?

One of my favorite transformers was The Fly from Archie Comics. Young Tommy Troy came into possession of a mystical ring that turned him into The Fly, complete with translucent wings, a buzz gun, and a goggle-eyed mask. He could call upon the powers of any insect, blinding criminals with a firefly glow or trapping them by spinning a web, and he could shatter windshields with his cricket hum. Inexplicably, The Fly could also become as tiny or gigantic as the situation demanded. His only weakness was the deadly pesticide chlordane. Like Billy Batson before him, Tommy Troy was an orphan, unwanted and abused. The wretched conditions of Tommy's life further dramatized his change from lowliness to greatness.

Do you wonder why Tommy reverted to his true identity at the end of every story? Why return to squalor and misery? Why not buy a business suit and remain the adult, powerful, good-looking Fly all the time?

In the world of superheroes and comic books, that's not how transformation works. The change is never permanent. The high-and-mighty identity is only a loaner. That's the rule.

## The Possibilities Within

Among the transformers, my hands-down, all-time favorite was a kid named Robby Reed who starred in a 1960s DC strip called *Dial H for Hero*. Robby found a mysterious alien device that looked like a telephone dial. After deciphering its weird markings, the youngster discovered that when he dialed H-E-R-O he became a superhero. Each time the H-dial turned, Robby changed into a different superhero. The possibilities were endless. Even if

Robby sometimes became an embarrassingly goofy hero (like Mighty Moppet!), he could hope for better luck next time. When the crisis passed or if Robby suffered serious injuries in his superhero guise, he simply dialed O-R-E-H to return to his real self.

I was so smitten with Robby and his H-dial that I carried a small bag in my pocket with slips of paper bearing the names of all Robby's heroes, updated each month with new entries. Whenever danger or tedium loomed, I dipped into the bag and transformed myself into someone powerful and bigger than life. Sometimes I'd let my little brother draw too, and our respective heroic identities would do battle.

I don't have the little bag anymore, but I still transform on occasion. Often the change takes place in the middle of a meeting that should have ended forty-five minutes earlier. Traffic jams are an invitation to become someone else for a while. Sometimes the whiff of spring flowers or the play of wind in my hair awakens such nameless longing that I simply have to fly for a while to get it out of my system. Oddly, no one ever notices the transformations, and I live a relatively normal life in spite of my many identities.

How about you? Be honest. You've never riffled your wallet hoping to find a 007 identification card or thumped away on an air guitar before an imaginary crowd of screaming admirers? Don't you sometimes trade places with Bill Gates or Tiger Woods or Oprah Winfrey? Have you tried out your boss's chair or longed to perform a perfect triple axel? You've never dreamed of being an ideal spouse who remembers anniversaries and dances like Rogers or Astaire? You don't wish you could be more like those TV parents who say such wise and helpful things to their children? You've never bought a self-help book promising to make you skinny or charismatic or spiritual?

You never dream of being more than you are? Then obviously you have an ideal life. All your dreams have become reality. You've maxed out your potential. You've achieved all your goals. Nothing remains beyond your reach. Congratulations. Every other mortal on the planet would love to know how you accomplished perfection!

Even the happiest and most well-adjusted people experience disappointment and discontent. However much we may like ourselves, we invariably find traits and quirks we dislike as well. We carry a secret list of personal changes we wish we could accomplish. For all our achievements, we harbor a nagging sense that we could and should be better than we are. There's a little Batman in all of us. For that matter, even Superman has been seeing a psychiatrist lately.

Not that change is out of reach. We constantly improve ourselves in all sorts of ways. We stop smoking. We join AA. We return to school. We become more caring parents and spouses. We learn how to say no. We lose weight. Maybe we even keep off that weight.

We take justifiable pride in these successes. Yet we find that beneath these outward changes we remain somehow the same. A skinny me is healthier and better looking, perhaps, but not necessarily happier. A sober me is far better than the alternative, but the empty place I used to fill with booze may still be empty. A better organized me will get more done, but efficiency will not satisfy my heart's hunger.

The old *Dial H for Hero* strip has recently been updated for a new millennium in a book titled *H-E-R-O*. The mysterious dial still bestows superpowers, but being a hero is tougher than it looks. In one storyline a chronic loser named Jerry gets hold of the dial. Sure enough, he transforms into one flying, muscle-bound character after another, but his adventures are disastrous. He halts a

96

weaving car, but the resulting crash nearly kills the drunk driver at the wheel. In trying to intimidate a teen drug dealer, Jerry loses his temper and puts the young man in the hospital. When Jerry attempts to save his girlfriend from an armed robber in an ice cream parlor, he gets the girl shot and nearly burns down the store.

At one point Jerry muses, "Even with super-powers I was still the same Jerry. Still nothing."[1] Surveying the wreckage in his wake, Jerry decides to kill himself, but he fails even at suicide.

In another storyline, a rising executive acquires the dial and becomes hooked on playing superhero. He neglects his family and his work so he can sneak off and use the dial. The hapless man is so addicted to dialing for powers that he scarcely notices the loss of his job or his wife's departure. In stark contrast, losing the dial leaves him in utter despair. The last we see of this formerly happy and successful man, he is weeping and hunched over like a craving junkie.

So superpowers do not necessarily make a superhero. If beauty is only skin deep, so are muscles, wings, and heat vision. External changes may not reach the inside. Superpowers transform what we can do but not who we are.

After well-meaning personal reforms and turning over whole volumes of new leaves, we still fall short of becoming our ideal selves. Performing better or looking better isn't sufficient; we long to become a new person. We covet a permanent change, to become new from the inside out, to change into our best selves, not a make-believe identity.

That's what God wants for us too. God loves us just as we are, but he also has big plans for you and me. As a look at Wonder Woman showed us, we are created beings with limits and mistakes galore, incomplete without the presence of our Maker.

But what we are is not what we will be. We are still becoming. The possibilities within us are beyond our loftiest imaginings and as vast and surprising as the towering oak sleeping within the acorn shell. You think a newsboy transformed into a superpowered champion is incredible? Wait until you see what God has in store.

## Transformed or Restored?

Of all the metamorphoses in the comic book universe, the story of the mighty Thor comes closest to God's plans for you and me. When Thor first appeared in *Journey into Mystery* #83 in 1962, he looked like nothing more than the latest addition to the long lineage of transforming superheroes. Stan Lee was creating a whole superhero universe from scratch. In the process of crafting Spider-Man, the Fantastic Four, the Hulk, Iron Man, and the X-Men, who can blame Lee for dipping into Norse mythology for a ready-made hero? To explain Thor's origin, Lee fell back on the tried and true transformation scenario. Or so it seemed at first.

Dr. Don Blake was vacationing in Norway when he stumbled across an impending alien invasion. In eluding the Saturnian aliens, Blake was trapped in a cave where he found a gnarled walking stick. In a moment of frustration, Blake struck the cane against a boulder. With a blinding flash, he became the embodiment of Thor, the ancient Norse thunder god. The walking stick took the form of Thor's invincible war hammer.

After making short work of the invading Saturnians, Thor discovered that stamping his weapon on the ground restored both hero and weapon to their mundane forms. Dr. Don Blake returned to New York, where he practiced medicine from nine to five, then moonlighted as a Norse deity.

98

For years Thor romped through fairly standard super-adventures. He maintained a secret identity and accumulated a motley gang of recurring enemies. Blake's nurse, Jane Foster, provided the requisite heartthrob. Thor even had a weakness that added suspense to his stories: After sixty seconds of separation from his hammer, the thunder god reverted to frail Don Blake.

Yet Thor was never the standard transforming hero. For one thing, he talked differently than Don Blake. The doctor spoke in standard American English, but Thor's speeches were well seasoned with archaic tenses lifted from the King James Bible. Thee's and thou's abounded. Stan Lee called it "neo-Shakespearean."

Clearly Don Blake's transformation into Thor didn't follow the usual pattern. Billy Batson could shout "Shazam!" and put on the body of Captain Marvel in a flash of lightning, yet inside that superb body, Billy Batson was still Billy Batson. He was stronger. He was faster. But he still thought and talked like Billy Batson; the heart beating in the breast of Captain Marvel was Billy Batson's heart.

In *The Dark Knight Strikes Again*, writer and artist Frank Miller reflects poignantly on Captain Marvel's emptiness apart from Billy Batson. Facing death, Captain Marvel muses on the hollowness of his identity, prepares for his own passing, and asks, "Where's a wish go? Where's a dream go when you wake up and you can't remember it? Nowhere."[2]

Captain Marvel was little more than a hero suit for Billy Batson to wear on special occasions. Thor's transformation was deeper. Thor thought and spoke in new ways. He knew things Blake didn't know. He had family ties and friendships that belonged to Thor alone. When Don Blake smacked his walking stick upon the New York pavement, he didn't just put on a new identity. In the deepest sense,

Blake became a new person who belonged to a bigger world with larger possibilities.

## Changed for Good

Thor made frequent visits to Asgard, the celestial city ruled by his father, Odin. Thor was at home in Asgard in a way Don Blake could never be anywhere. Thor belonged to a circle of heroes and cherished friends; even Don Blake's relationships and community transformed when he became Thor.

Something odd was going on, but nobody understood what until Stan Lee and Jack Kirby pulled the rug out from under fans in *Thor* #159. Everything we'd believed about Thor since his first appearance six years earlier turned out to be false. Well, almost everything. Actually, we were right about Thor. It was Don Blake we were wrong about, because Don Blake didn't really exist.

Thor had grown up in Asgard and lived there for thousands of years. He was the most powerful warrior in the realm, and his prowess made him boastful and headstrong. He broke treaties and brawled in taverns. Odin feared his son was becoming arrogant and prideful. In order to teach Thor humility, Odin turned the thunder god into a mortal and sent him to Earth to live in the guise of Don Blake.

Thor arrived on Earth as a twentysomething Don Blake with no past and no history. Odin's enchantment prevented Blake from wondering about the absence of memories or family ties. The limping Don Blake worked his way through medical school and became a surgeon. He lived among mortals, easing their suffering and healing their illnesses but never dreaming that his human life was pretense.

When the time was ripe, Odin manipulated the events that led to Don Blake's recovery of the magic hammer. Whenever

Blake became Thor, readers thought he was putting on a heroic guise for a while, just like Tommy Troy rubbing the magic fly ring or Robby Reed dialing H-E-R-O. When Thor reverted to Don Blake, we assumed he was returning to his true self. We were wrong. Don Blake was only temporary. Thor was the true and permanent identity all along.

Comic fans believe in transformation. So do Christians. We believe God is transforming us into sons and daughters of unimaginable glory. As soon as we put our faith in Jesus Christ, we become new creatures—not the same old people with some cosmetic changes, but fresh creations.

From eternity this has always been God's great plan for us. "For those God foreknew he also predestined to be conformed to the likeness of his Son" (Rom. 8:29). Before time began, God already loved us. Before we truly existed, God had already appointed us for an amazing destiny.

What is that destiny? God intends for us to be transformed into the image of Christ. The God who formed us from the clay is even now shaping us into the likeness of his own Son. God's gracious goal for each of us is that we become "mature and full grown in the Lord, measuring up to the full stature of Christ . . . becoming more and more in every way like Christ" (Eph. 4:13, 15 NLT).

This is bigger than Captain Marvel, bigger than magic words, H-dials, and fly rings. Comic book characters may turn into heroes, but Christians are being transformed into the likeness of the Lord and Savior of the universe. Like Thor, we are being changed into the image of the divine.

But unlike Thor, we are not transformed entirely in a single moment. Rather, God is gradually changing us, degree by degree. The reality of our new creation unfolds over a lifetime and even beyond. In the best comic book tradition, our transformation is an unearned blessing, grace pure and simple. Our metamorphosis into the likeness of

Who Needs a Superhero?

the risen Lord is entirely God's gift, but God invites us to cooperate in the unwrapping of that gift. The Bible encourages us to strive for lives that reflect our high calling. "You must display a new nature because you are a new person, created in God's likeness—righteous, holy, and true" (Eph. 4:24 NLT).

God calls us to lifelong growth, an upward path that brings us ever nearer to our goal of becoming like Christ. God gives us the growth, but we are free to either claim or stunt that growth.

## Becoming Our Highest Selves

Do you remember the Marvel hero Goliath? His real name was Henry Pym, a scientist who discovered a technique for shrinking himself to insect size. Donning a uniform and a cybernetic helmet for communicating with six-legged creatures, Pym became the adventurer Ant-Man. After joining the Avengers, Pym refined his abilities and gained the power to grow to a height of twenty-five feet. The scientist changed his name to Giant-Man and became a powerhouse who played a key role in the Avengers.

Then one day Giant-Man got stuck. In the process of returning to his normal size, Giant-Man's height froze at ten feet. He lost the ability to change his size. He adopted the name Goliath and continued to fight beside the Avengers, but he was less impressive. As a hero he had stopped growing—in both senses. Eventually Pym found a way to return to his natural height, but he was never again as effective as he had been in his younger, growing years. Adopting yet another name and costume as Yellow Jacket, Pym again became a shrinking hero.

For all practical purposes he shrank into oblivion.

102

Invisible Girl, the female member of the Fantastic Four, represents quite a different story. After exposure to cosmic radiation, Sue Storm was able to turn invisible at will. Frankly, Invisible Girl was little more than window dressing in the early days of the Fantastic Four—usually unseen window dressing. Invisibility wasn't much help in a serious fight with powerful villains. Typically Sue Storm tripped fleeing enemies or jostled their aim or threw a crucial lever at the critical moment. Yawn . . .

However, Sue Storm grew. She developed the power to turn other people and objects invisible, an ability handy for deceiving or confusing foes. She then discovered the power to create invisible force fields. With these force fields the Invisible Girl could trap her opponents and protect her teammates. Many times an invisible force field was all that lay between the Fantastic Four and destruction. Eventually the Invisible Girl even mastered her power as an offensive weapon. With patient practice, Sue Storm learned to focus her force field in spheres she could hurl as unseen missiles. From a weak link she developed into a formidable and heroic person. To symbolize her growing confidence and ability the Invisible Girl changed her name: She was stronger, better, wiser—and, now, the Invisible Woman.

The stuck and stagnant Goliath or the growing, maturing Invisible Woman—which character expresses God's hopes for you and me? Survival in a rut or life on the peaks?

God wants us to live abundantly. We are flawed and imperfect creatures, but God loves us as we are. That love is changing us into something glorious. God turns creepy-crawlers into monarch butterflies, gas particles into stars, and coal into diamonds. Why is it so difficult to believe he can transform his children into the likeness of Christ?

Contrary to the opinion of many who should know better, Christianity is not about becoming informed, as if memorizing a creed or accepting a set of doctrines were the whole of God's will for us. Nor is Christianity about becoming morally reformed. Our behavior matters, but we diminish God when we pretend that Christianity is merely a code of conduct or a string of rules.

Simply put, Christianity is about becoming transformed.

Like Dr. Donald Blake's earthly life, our time in this world is the prelude for a glorious eternity. Our mortal reality is the preparation for becoming our true and highest selves. We are sojourners on earth with one foot here and the other in a bright and heavenly home. Even if we are ignorant or skeptical of our destiny, God's plan is sure. Our transformation is certain. God has promised that "you will share in his divine nature" (2 Peter 1:4 NLT).

The story of Thor became more exciting when we found out the truth of his identity. Our lives become more exciting too when we understand who we are and who we will be. The news of God's transforming love is almost too good to be true. We sometimes have trouble believing the future God has in store for us.

When I catch myself doubting God's plans for me, I turn to a wonderful prayer I learned from my friend Cec Murphey. It's a pithy prayer, and it opens my heart to God's incredible possibilities: "Loving God, show me the truth about myself, no matter how beautiful it may be."[3]

# 8 Spider-Man
## Saved for Service

Peter Parker was the stereotypical comic book nerd: a thin, geeky, bespectacled bookworm, the butt of every school joke, a kid who never had a date or went to a dance. When the other kids drove off for a pizza, Peter headed for the new exhibit at the Science Hall.

Who could guess it would be the exhibit and not a dance that would change Peter Parker's life forever? In the Science Hall, he's bitten by a radioactive spider. The once timid Parker now finds fate has given him arachnid powers: the proportionate strength of a spider, the ability to climb walls, superhuman reflexes, and a strange "spider sense" that warns him of impending danger.

It doesn't occur to Peter that these gifts could save lives and render good. He's too focused on himself. *Finally*, Peter determines, *proof for my schoolmates that the chronic loser has become a winner*. He designs web-shooters that spray nearly unbreakable webbing from dispensers on his wrists. Before venturing into the world, he dons a mask, lest he look foolish in public. Even his doting guardians, Uncle Ben and Aunt May, don't know about Peter's new powers and double identity as he uses his spider-powers to defeat a wrestler in an exhibition match.

The win nets Peter Parker a quick one hundred bucks and a spot on television. Life seems to be turning around. Unfortunately, Parker's attitude shows no improvement. An incident at the television studio reveals the selfish shallowness of the teenager. As Parker pauses in a hallway, a criminal runs down the corridor in his direction. A pursuing police officer calls for a hand, but the teenager watches indifferently as the thug sprints past and escapes in an elevator.

"What's with you, mister?" the angry cop confronts Parker. "All you hadda do was trip him or just hold him for a minute!"

Peter Parker's answer reveals how deeply he's been hurt and angered by years of ridicule at school: "Sorry, pal! That's your job! I'm through being pushed around—by anyone! From now on I only look out for number one—that means—me!"[1]

In both the comic book world and the real world, life often hinges on just such apparently insignificant decisions. In the weeks that follow, Spider-Man becomes a sensation in stage shows and in television appearances, until one evening he returns from a performance to find a patrol car parked in front of his home. A police officer breaks the news: A burglar has shot and killed beloved Uncle Ben, then escaped to a nearby warehouse on the waterfront where he's holding the police at bay.

A tearful Peter Parker dresses in his Spider-Man costume and sets off to capture the killer. Slipping through the police cordon, he disarms the crook and punches him unconscious. Only then does Spider-Man get a clear look at the killer's face; this is the same fugitive who ran past Parker weeks before at the television studio. The teenager's irresponsible behavior allowed the criminal to remain at large. Because of such selfishness Uncle Ben was dead.

The heartbroken youth wanders into the night, head bowed and shoulders slumped. The story's closing caption suggests that Spider-Man is finally prepared to accept his rightful place as a hero: "And a lean, silent figure slowly fades into the gathering darkness, aware at last that in this world, with great power there must also come great responsibility."[2]

## Superhero Know-How

With Uncle Ben's death Spider-Man learns slowly and painfully what most superheroes grasp intuitively and immediately. Take, for instance, the Fantastic Four.

In their first issue, four American would-be astronauts have crash-landed on Earth after an ill-fated attempt to become the first humans in outer space. They walk away from the ruined rocket miraculously uninjured but heavily exposed to mysterious cosmic rays. Within minutes their bodies demonstrate the incredible effects of the radiation. Johnny Storm bursts into flame. His sister Susan becomes momentarily invisible. Reed Richards discovers his limbs have become elastic and stretchable. Ben Grimm, the gruff pilot of the rocket, turns into a monstrous figure of tremendous strength.

When the shock subsides, Reed Richards suggests that the foursome consider the implications of their superpowers.

Before Richards can get very far, the irascible Ben Grimm, soon to be known as the Thing, interrupts him: "You don't have to make a speech, big shot! We understand! We've gotta use that power to help mankind, right?"[3]

The foursome has just walked away from a rocket crash uninjured, survived a potentially lethal exposure to radiation, and received formidable abilities in the bargain. Both blessed and empowered, they understand the gifts they've been given. They know they're called to give something back to the world. They resolve to use their powers to aid others.

The Fantastic Four's origin follows a particularly common comic book pattern: the process of peril-power-promise. Here's how it works: Our hero faces a crisis that threatens to destroy him. Instead, our hero emerges with superhuman abilities and vows to use them for good.

Christian life follows a similar path. The initials differ for steps in the process, but the pattern is nearly identical: sin-salvation-service.

Compare the process. Christians know humanity is locked in a struggle with the power of sin, a force as wild and ruthless as the Hulk. No best effort will win that battle, and neither personal goodness nor wealth nor success can save us. Only the truth will set humanity free—the truth of our need and the truth of God's love offered in Jesus Christ.

Like Superman, Jesus left his place in heaven and came into our world to take his stand beside us. If we have faith in Jesus, we know his gracious death and victorious resurrection saves us, and by this we understand two things that even Superman cannot deliver. Christ has saved us *from* something, namely sin and death, and Christ has saved us *for* something.

For anyone who's ever wondered "what?" the answer is in those words spoken by the Fantastic Four's Grimm, aka the Thing, after his own salvation from death.

Years ago at a convention I asked Fantastic Four creator Stan Lee to write that short speech in his own hand on a piece of Marvel superhero stationery. I later framed those simple sentences and hung them on the wall above my desk where I read them often—an unvarnished reminder, that bears repeating, of how Christians should use the gifts of God.

"You don't have to make a speech, big shot! We understand! We've gotta use that power to help mankind, right?"[4]

## Being Good and Good for Something

Sin-salvation-service and peril-power-promise both lead to the same action: devoting oneself to a lifelong mission of gratitude. Unfortunately, many Christians overlook the final step in the process as if a profession of faith in Jesus finishes their stories.

Quite the contrary is true. The Christian story has barely begun when Christ enters our lives. "For we are what he has made us," Paul explained to the first Christians, "created in Christ Jesus for good works, which God prepared beforehand to be our way of life" (Eph. 2:10 NRSV).

If we progress no further than sin-salvation, God's purpose for us is frustrated. Without service, our discipleship remains sadly incomplete.

Superman beautifully expresses this healthy theology of gifts when he says, "I look upon my powers as a gift, not mine alone but for anyone who needs them."[5]

By his next appearance in *Spider-Man* #1, Peter Parker also accepts this truth and the calling to serve.[6] He risks his life to rescue an astronaut in a runaway space capsule and in his second story thwarts the Chameleon, a master spy. Finally Spider-Man has completed the superhero pattern of peril-power-promise. Though learned at a bitter cost, the idea that "with great power comes great responsibility" has become Spider-Man's unofficial slogan.

What about those of us with less-fantastical, less-apparent superpowers?

109

I recall a story about a worship service of African Christians. As worshipers came forward one by one to bring their offerings to God, some brought money and others brought homegrown vegetables or handmade goods. One impoverished woman caught the true spirit of giving and danced to the front of the room, set the offering plate on the floor, and stood in it.

She knew the truth: Once Christ has claimed us for his own at the price of his blood, we have a great responsibility and joy. We offer all we are and all we have in his service. We not only need to be good; we also need to be good for something.

"What good is it, my brothers and sisters, if you say you have faith but do not have works? . . . If a brother or sister is naked and lacks daily food, and one of you says to them, 'Go in peace; keep warm and eat your fill,' yet you do not supply their bodily needs, what is the good of that? So faith by itself, if it has no works, is dead" (James 2:14–17 NRSV).

Some of us have grown up vicariously enjoying the accomplishments of superheroes, but we ordinary mortals also have opportunities to change the world. We don't need superpowers or unlimited resources to make a difference. What happens, then, when we live out the full pattern of sin-salvation-service? Could our efforts improve the lives of people around us and grow the world closer to God's vision for humanity?

Consider exercising a fairly modest gift like a love for comic books.

Huh? Can such a gift improve the world?

Many comic book collectors periodically purge their collections of duplicates, unwanted issues, and lesser quality books. I have friends who regularly donate those surplus comics to local literacy programs. Imagine the impact of helping a youngster master reading skills that will shape his opportunities for decades to come.

For several years I attended a major comic book convention that was organized as a fundraiser for the March of Dimes. Because a fan saw the potential to use his hobby as a means to generate income for medical research, tens of thousands of dollars were raised over several years.

On a recent visit to my comic book store I noticed a drawing of Daredevil by local professional David Mack. The art was for sale to benefit the victims of a nearby house fire.

Johnny Hart frequently includes Christian messages in his newspaper strip *B.C.*

The late Al Hartley, longtime artist for Archie Comics, used to create Christian comic books using the Archie characters.

Despite pressure from TV executives, Charles Schulz remained true to his Christian convictions while creating *A Charlie Brown Christmas*. The result is one of television's most enduring and endearing expressions of the real meaning of Christmas.

Inker Gary Martin was contracted to finish the artwork for *Nexus: God Con*. Martin was troubled by the book's theology, especially the treatment of Jesus in the story. With reservations Martin fulfilled his work on the art, and a thoughtful editor allowed Martin to offer his Christian testimony in the letter column.

A close friend of mine combined his faith with his love for comics to write Sunday school comic books for a denominational publisher.

Alex Ross provided painted art for the touching *Superman: Peace on Earth*, a story we visited in chapter 5. That book told the story of Superman's failed efforts to alleviate world hunger. Fittingly, Ross sold the original artwork from that book and donated the proceeds to charity. He's done likewise with art from several subsequent books in the same series.

I wouldn't presume to know the religious convictions of each person I've mentioned in this list, but in every case these ordinary people have used a passion for comics to better the world.

Admittedly, comic collecting is a less formidable gift than flight or super strength, but that's the point. If God can use a mania for comic books, God can use any gift we offer. When we lay even our least promising gifts at God's feet, God has a knack for blessing their use. It's a principle that even a child can discover.

At a recent outdoor concert, an orchestra conductor brought a kindergarten boy on stage for a bit of showmanship. Handing the boy his baton, the conductor instructed the boy to swing the wand in a strong downbeat. The boy hesitated, but with the conductor's encouragement lashed the baton through the air. Immediately a drum roll began, the orchestra rose and launched into the national anthem, and the audience immediately came to its feet. The wide-eyed five-year-old was amazed at the results of one swing of the baton.

Even small acts of faithfulness to carry out the humble tasks within our reach yield far-reaching results when God blesses our efforts. If we resolve to use the gifts God's given, he will take care of the results.

## Doing What Needs to Be Done, Regardless

In what's perhaps my favorite comic book story, Spider-Man trails Dr. Octopus, who has stolen a radioactive medication called Iso-36. That serum is the only hope to save the life of Spider-Man's hospitalized Aunt May. Spider-Man tracks Dr. Octopus to his lair on the floor of the sea. During a brutal slugfest, the underwater hideout partially collapses. The villain makes good his escape, but Spider-Man is pinned beneath tons of debris.

*Amazing Spider-Man* #32 ended on one of the greatest cliffhangers in comic book history. Twenty feet out of reach is the radioactive serum on which Aunt May's life depends. Water pours into the damaged building. Spider-Man struggles vainly against the massive weight bearing down on him. After days of relentless effort, the young man is exhausted. He can't budge the debris. The rising water level will soon submerge the trapped hero. All seems lost. Spider-Man and Aunt May are apparently doomed.

Waiting for the next issue was the longest four weeks of my life. When *Amazing Spider-Man* #33 finally arrived, I couldn't wait to get it home. Instead I sat down on the sidewalk in front of the drugstore and read it on the spot.

As the story opens, Spider-Man strives again and again against the weight of the wreckage, but to no avail. He drifts in and out of consciousness, seeing visions of Aunt May in her hospital bed.

The water rises and Spider-Man gathers his strength for one final effort. The debris shifts infinitesimally. The hero heaves again, and the weight moves another fraction of an inch.

"Within my body is the strength of many men!" Spider-Man declares. "And now, I've got to call on all that strength—all the power—that I possess! I must prove equal to the task—I must be worthy of that strength—or else I don't deserve it!"[7]

As the scene unfolds, the panels grow larger and larger. On the verge of blacking out, Spider-Man expends the last iota of his strength.

To my dying day I will remember that full-page drawing of a triumphant Spider-Man rising to his feet and pressing tons of metal on outstretched arms.

What happened? At the end of one issue he couldn't lift the weight, and then in the next he could. Isn't that cheating? No. Spider-Man made up his mind to use his abilities to their fullest. In the moment of trial, Peter Parker discovered his gifts were enough to do what needed to be done.

You've probably had the same experience, albeit under less dramatic circumstances. As a young pastor I was terrified that I might say or do the wrong thing in a crisis situation. I pumped one of my experienced colleagues for the right Scripture to read after a stillbirth and the best prayer to offer after a suicide and the most comforting words to use while waiting for the outcome of risky surgery. After an hour of this interrogation, my friend cut off my remaining questions.

"Listen," he told me, "serving God means showing up and making yourself available for God's use. You won't always have the right words or the perfect prayer. That's okay. The people you're helping will later forget what passage you recited or what you said in the prayer, but they will always remember that you were there. If you'll just show up, God will find a way to use you and your gifts."

I've taken that advice to heart. I never feel adequate to the task when I have to help a family through a suicide or an accidental death, but I show up and God finds a way to use me. When we offer ourselves in God's service, God doesn't guarantee us success in every venture, but he will provide sufficient strength to do whatever we are truly called to do. Whether our gifts are great or small, in God's gracious hands those gifts will be enough.

We often have trouble believing that our gifts are sufficient for God's purposes. Maybe you wish you had different gifts to use. Can I confess a secret envy? I've always been good with words, but that wasn't the gift I wanted.

I longed to be an artist. I yearned to draw. I imagined my work gracing book covers and hanging in galleries. In fact, I can't draw a crooked line without making a mess.

Spider-Man probably wishes he could fly instead of having to swing around the New York skyline on synthetic cobwebs. Maybe he'd love to swap his wall-crawling power for X-ray vision. No matter. We don't get to choose our gifts and talents. We can improve and hone our gifts, or we can minimize and neglect them. But that's as far as our choices reach.

Sometimes God's plan is different from ours. When that happens, our best course is to use the gifts we have, trusting God to make them count. "For if the eagerness is there, the gift is acceptable according to what one has—not according to what one does not have" (2 Cor. 8:12 NRSV).

Do you remember the FedEx commercial spoofing the popular movie *Castaway* that aired during the 2003 Super Bowl? A deliveryman knocks on the door of a suburban house. When a woman answers, the man proudly hands over a package. He tells the woman he's been stranded on a deserted island for years. Through many hardships and privations he held on to this package planning for the day he could deliver it in person. The woman accepts the package with thanks, but before the door closes the former castaway asks the woman what's in the package.

The woman assures him it's nothing particularly important, just a few odds and ends: a satellite telephone, a global positioning device, a compass, a water purifier, and some seeds.

When we Christians don't exercise our gifts, we're just like the castaway who refuses to unwrap what God has placed within his reach. We hobble through life, struggle with circumstances, and cripple ourselves because we don't take hold of the gifts God intends for us. When we neglect our gifts, we reject the very resources an all-wise God has provided for abundant living. Overlooking our gifts impoverishes us and makes life harder than it need be.

On the other hand, nothing else is so fulfilling as faithfully exercising our gifts to God's glory. This path leads to our greatest contentment and joy. We do our children such a disservice when we encourage the belief that making money is the chief end of life. Certainly we need to provide for the necessities, but our lives mean more and accomplish more when serving God is our first priority.

Not that our gifts will necessarily yield wealth and success. Especially in the early years of the Spider-Man character, the more Spider-Man serves the world with his powers, the more frequently he's branded a menace and outlaw. He's often short of money. His Spider-Man identity also complicates his family life and his friendships. Of course, these frustrations anger the young man, yet Peter Parker doesn't mothball his costume. He can't turn his back on his gifts, in spite of his personal sacrifices and the world's ingratitude. Once Parker tastes the thrill of being Spider-Man, a nine-to-five existence seems bland and banal.

It's the same for us. The world may reward us with money when we deny our gifts for the sake of fitting the expectations of others, but using our gifts thankfully and faithfully yields what money can't purchase: peace with God and peace with ourselves.

I met a woman at a Christian writer's conference who used to work for a prestigious advertising agency in New York. Her income was six figures, and her future looked dazzling. She told me, "I took a long time to discover I wasn't happy in the ad business. I was using my best talents to sell mouthwash and underwear. I was going to waste! Although I hadn't been in church for years, I went to a Christian retreat center to think about my values and priorities. I guess

116

God got hold of me there. I never went back to the agency." Today she uses her gifts in the service of Christ, supporting causes she believes in. She writes for several Christian ministries: a newsletter, a humor column, occasional articles and brochures. "I'm not making much money," she says, smiling brightly, "but I'm making a great life."

When we devote ourselves to serving God with our talents and abilities, we unknowingly become role models. When others see us using our gifts, they're often inspired and encouraged to use their own. In the DC universe, Superman is the ultimate role model and the inspiration for a generation of heroes. In one story Wonder Woman phones Superman in his Clark Kent identity to thank him for advice he recently shared with her. Clark Kent deflects the compliment with a chuckle and offers to pay for dinner the next time the two heroes get together. Wonder Woman smiles and thinks to herself, "Clark has no idea what an inspiration he is to me and others."[8]

That's how heroes affect us—even from the comic page into real life, like mine for example. After being a Superman fan for years, I briefly corresponded in 1987 with Superman's creator, the late Jerry Siegel. I decided I should tell this man how much I'd enjoyed his work over the years. Siegel replied in a series of letters, always warm and humble.

"I regret that years ago, I missed seeing you, when you were very young, with that towel tied around your neck, standing in a dramatic crouch, fists clenched, poised and eager to leap up, up, and away to the rescue of suffering humanity," Siegel wrote in one letter. He added, "I am glad that Superman's mission to help those in need inspired you to do likewise."[9]

Should I be embarrassed that a comic book character is one of my role models? I'm not. Whether on the printed page or in my own neighborhood, I'm constantly inspired by those who use their gifts gladly and thankfully to build a better world. Ordinary people abound with heroism. I could make a long list of quiet, overlooked people who have inspired me by their faithfulness; most of these people would be shocked that I find anything heroic in their lives. True heroism rarely involves front-page rescues or superhuman achievements. A hero is anyone who uses his or her gifts to do what needs to be done in the service of God's world.

We have gifts, and we have a calling. Jesus has saved us from sin and for service. God has gifted us not only for our own sake but also for the benefit of a needy world. We have work to do, and by God's grace we have the means to do it.

Or to paraphrase a certain web-spinning wall crawler, "With great blessing comes great responsibility."

# Daredevil
# Discernment

**A**t first glance, Daredevil appears to lack the stuff from which superheroes are made. Where the mutant hero Havok can fire bolts of sizzling energy plasma from his hands, Daredevil can taste the additives in his diet cola. Where Hulk can press more than one hundred tons, Daredevil can identify perfume from two blocks away. Where Quicksilver can run at speeds in excess of 175 miles per hour, Daredevil reads newsprint with his fingertips. Where Thor emerges intact from a nuclear blast, Daredevil responds to being shot by a handgun by . . . bleeding freely and passing out?

Huh? This is a superhero?

Truly Daredevil's not your ordinary superhero. He's no stronger or hardier than an ordinary athlete. His most sophisticated weapon is a cane folded into a billy club. He lives in Hell's Kitchen. And his sole superpower? Heightened senses. Right. While the ability to hear a pin drop might sell telephones, it hardly seems to qualify Daredevil for leading a war on crime.

Oh, and did I mention he's blind?

Hero-worthy or not, Daredevil remains one of Marvel's longest-running characters. Since the sightless hero debuted in 1964, he's attracted some of the medium's most gifted writers and artists—from golden age greats like Bill Everett and Wally Wood to contemporary wonderboys Kevin Smith, Brian Bendis, and David Mack. The best of the *Daredevil* issues, created by Frank Miller, are as good as comic books get, and ol' Hornhead is one of the more popular superheroes on the silver screen.

So what's the appeal of this urban adventurer?

His origin is a variation on the hero-seeking-revenge theme. Young Matt Murdock wants to grow up to be just like his father, the rough-and-tumble prizefighter "Battling" Jack Murdock. But the elder Murdock had promised Matt's dying mother that he would help the boy get an education and make something of himself.

At his father's insistence, Matt applies himself single-mindedly to his studies. He hits the books so diligently that he earns the enmity of the local bullies, who mockingly nickname the bookworm "Daredevil." Unbeknownst to his peers or father, Matt sneaks away from the books to the gym for exhausting workouts on the bag, the rings, and the beam. As he grows, Matt develops himself both mentally and physically.

He's well on his way to fulfilling his father's vicarious ambitions when an accident nearly derails his plans. Matt sees a blind man crossing the street in front of a runaway truck and springs into action. Leaping forward, Matt pushes the blind man to safety but is struck in the process. On impact, a barrel tumbles from the truck bed, breaks open, and splashes Matt's face with radioactive waste.

When he wakes up in the hospital, Matt Murdock is blind. The combination of the impact and the radioactive chemicals has robbed him of sight. However, the accident has heightened Matt's remaining senses, granting him superhuman

120

perceptions of a rich world of smells, tastes, and sounds unimaginable to ordinary people. The exposure to radiation has also bestowed upon him a mysterious radar sense that allows him to detect objects, movement, and distance. Matt keeps his newfound abilities secret and redoubles his efforts at both school and the gym.

Meanwhile, "Battling" Jack Murdock has trouble raising money for his son's college education. In desperation, the over-the-hill fighter hooks up with a crooked promoter called the Fixer. But Jack Murdock defies the Fixer's orders to throw a fight one evening when Matt is in the audience. Eager to make his son proud, the aging boxer defeats a much younger opponent. The Fixer retaliates by having the elder Murdock gunned down in the street.

In spite of his grief, Matt finishes his education and graduates as valedictorian of his class. He opens a law office with school chum Foggy Nelson to fight for justice in the legal system. But Matt's victories are rendered hollow by his father's unavenged murder. He begins to craft a plan. He dons a costume, dubs himself Daredevil (transforming the childhood taunt into a title of pride), and vows to use his super senses to track down his father's killers. He soon sends the gunman to jail. He sees the Fixer die too—dropping from a heart attack in an effort to flee our avenging hero.

Because young Matt Murdock promised his father he'd make his way in the world using his mind, not his fists, the second identity of Daredevil offers the young man a way to keep his promise and still indulge his adventurous yearnings. Matt Murdock the attorney will fulfill his father's dreams for a respectable, peaceful life. On the other hand, Daredevil will be a separate persona carrying on the good fight in the spirit of heroic Jack Murdock.

## Beyond the Illusions

Imagine, if you can, the world in which Daredevil lives. His ears reveal the activities hidden behind locked doors as well as conversations in passing subway trains and termites munching through hidden joists. As he walks the New York streets, his nose tells him what each person had for lunch, what laundry detergent they favor, and who owns pets. A handshake is an instant diagnostic tool revealing temperature, blood pressure, pulse rate, muscle tone, and stress levels.

Daredevil reads the level of humidity and shifts in atmospheric pressure as clearly as a billboard. The pounding of an accelerated heartbeat and the heat radiating from a flushed face tell him when someone is masking anger. He can hear which piston isn't firing in a passing car, smell the efficiency of the catalytic converter, and feel the vibration of a tire out of alignment—from five hundred yards away.

In short, Daredevil is in tune with the world, uniquely and fully aware of events unfolding around him. He looks beyond the appearance of life and experiences undiluted reality. While most people pass through their days in a fog of ignorance and indifference, Daredevil perceives the truth of things. Both by gift and by discipline, he continually practices the art of discernment.

Daredevil's powers may be unusual by comic book standards, but they represent the thing to which all mature Christians aspire. Call it insight, heightened understanding, or the ability to differentiate between good and evil, but by whatever name, these gifts are like the ancient Christian discipline known as practicing discernment. Seeing the world more clearly, recognizing God's guidance, making decisions based on an understanding of the truth—these

are other ways of describing discernment. It means looking beyond illusions, deceptions, distractions, and wishful
thinking. Discernment allows one a deeper reality, a way
to get at the truth hidden beneath the surface of things.

Writing to the Corinthian church, which was a congregation of Christians surrounded by false gods, immorality,
and competing demands for loyalty, the apostle Paul tells
his friends, "You know that when you were still pagans you
were led astray and swept along in worshiping speechless
idols. So I want you to know how to discern what is truly
from God" (1 Cor. 12:2–3 NLT).

Phrases like "led astray" and "swept along" describe our
common experiences too. Fads and trends can carry away
the best of us with the marching multitudes. Glittering
promises beguile, empty values gull us into exchanging the
precious for the paltry—and all because we fail to discern
what truly comes from God and leads to God.

We speak glibly of setting proper priorities in life, but
prioritizing is impossible without discernment. Estab-
lishing priorities means selecting wisely from the myriad
options the world offers us. We must see reality clearly in
order to distinguish between the truly important and the
merely urgent. The practice of discernment teaches us to
differentiate the worthwhile from the worthless, the time-
less from the timely. Without discernment we can frame
no answer for the prophet's challenge: "Why spend money
on what is not bread, and your labor on what does not
satisfy?" (Isa. 55:2).

The matter of priorities is the crucial question for Daredevil. In every moment of the day the blind hero is barraged
by countless odors, tastes, sounds, and tactile sensations.
He must unceasingly sort and evaluate the tidal wave of
impressions and information that sweeps through his
senses. Without the ability to choose a few pressing mat-

ters from the millions of distractions, Daredevil would be paralyzed by the sheer clamor of existence.

In fact, when Matt Murdock first gained his powers, the constant, agonizing sensory input nearly drove him mad. The young man might not have survived except for the arrival of a mysterious teacher named Stick. The unshaven and ragged Stick was part Zen master, part Eastern sensei, and part pool hustler. Like Matt Murdock, Stick was blind. He had trained his remaining senses to an amazing level of awareness, and he stepped in to rescue Matt Murdock from drowning in a churning sea of experience.

With Stick's help, Matt Murdock gradually learned to sift through his impressions, disregarding the irrelevant and attending to the crucial. Once Daredevil mastered his new powers, he acquired the discipline to "monitor" thousands of bits of information yet focus only on those few that required his attention. Now the hero scans the world around him, continually judging what's important and what's not. He holds fast to a very few things and discards the rest. Deceiving him is nearly impossible. The throb of a rising pulse, the odor of perspiration, and the quaver of vocal modulation are the telltale signs of a lie. Informers waste their breath trying to mislead Daredevil. Their deceptions blaze like neon before his heightened senses. No wonder attorney Matt Murdock is an esteemed interrogator of witnesses. He immediately recognizes the slightest departure from the truth.

## Learn to Discern

We mere mortals lack Daredevil's advantages. We must muddle through life without a built-in lie detector. We must strain our ears to catch the whisper of love through the strident blare of selfishness. We must weigh the opportunities in a day and pursue those that lead toward the kingdom of God. We must learn to mute the clamor of the false idols so we can attend to the voice of the true God.

Discernment cultivates an aptitude for apprehending the truth—and we can learn to perceive the truth, at least as much of the truth as we need to keep our lives on course. The wisdom of Scripture explored through centuries of Christian spirituality offers tools for the practice of discernment. Any Christian willing to make a persistent effort can learn the skills and disciplines that reveal God's guiding presence in our daily Babel. With perseverance we can train ourselves to sift the valuable from the worthless.

The first step is simply the earnest desire to perceive God's guidance in our lives. Just the honest longing to hear God's voice is a giant stride toward discernment. Prophesying about the Messiah, Isaiah writes, "He will not judge by what he sees with his eyes, or decide by what he hears with his ears" (Isa. 11:3). Isaiah predicts that the Messiah will base his actions on realities beyond the perception of physical vision and hearing.

The followers of the Messiah seek to do likewise. The reality we can see and touch is the tiniest tip of the iceberg. Beneath the surface of things lies a vast and far-reaching spiritual realm. An Old Testament story tells how the King of Aram sent a large detachment of troops to capture the Israelite prophet Elisha. During the night the soldiers surrounded the city of Dothan where Elisha was staying. Elisha's servant was terrified when he spied the encircling army the next morning, but Elisha encouraged the fearful man. "'Don't be afraid,' the prophet answered. 'Those who are with us are more than those who are with them'" (2 Kings 6:16).

This answer bewildered the servant, for he was seeing the situation only on the surface level. Elisha, however, was peering into deeper spiritual reality. Elisha then asked God to open the eyes of his servant so that he might truly see. When the servant's eyes were opened to the unseen realm, he suddenly beheld a vast heavenly army of fiery chariots and angelic troops. Elisha might be trapped within the feeble circle of Aramean soldiers, but those troops were in turn surrounded by the blazing hosts of heaven.

The world is rife with the power and presence of God, but most people never notice. This is not a failing of the senses but of the heart. Admittedly, some perceptions are beyond our reach. No matter how we strain, we cannot hear the high-pitched tones that prick up the ears of our dogs. Nor will we ever see colors in the ultraviolet spectrum as the honeybees do. God did not build us for such sensations, but our Creator has equipped us for spiritual awareness. "You will seek me and find me when you seek me with all your heart" (Jer. 29:13). The acknowledgment of an unseen reality prepares us to experience that realm. The heart-deep longing for God's presence is the first step in finding God in the world.

The second step is learning to pay attention. Think again of young Matt Murdock struggling in vain to sort out the thousands of smells, tastes, and sounds battering his consciousness. Only by great effort does Daredevil learn to sift through the endless messages and give his attention to those that matter. In the movie *Daredevil*, we see the beleaguered hero floating in a sensory deprivation tank just for a few moments of peace.

Now consider your typical day. Is it so different from Matt Murdock's personal chaos? Are you not constantly besieged by ringing telephones, crying children, sirens, pagers, deadlines, home maintenance, and overdue bills? Given a blank page you could easily extend this clamorous list, couldn't you? We live in sensory overload. The clamor

126

of people, situations, and crises demanding our attention never subsides. We're too busy keeping our chins above water to peer beneath the surface. In the midst of the daily commotion, who can discern spiritual realities?

You can.

So can I.

If we want to, we can learn to listen for God's voice among the many voices. First Kings 19 tells the story of Elijah the prophet, who had taken refuge in a mountain cave to escape from those who sought to kill him. Longing for a word from God, Elijah stood in the mouth of the cave and waited for God's message.

As Elijah stood there at attention, a cyclonic wind pummeled the mountain and shattered great boulders, but the prophet ignored the storm. God was not in the wind. Then an earthquake shook the mountain. Elijah fought to keep his feet, but the shaking did not distract him. God was not in the earthquake. When the tremors subsided, a ferocious fire scoured the face of the mountain. Elijah kept his vigil while the blaze roared and died. God was not in the fire.

After the storm, the earthquake, and the inferno, silence descended upon the mountain. In the stillness Elijah heard a faint whisper. In reverence he pulled his cloak over his face and turned to meet the Lord, for the prophet knew this still, small voice represented nothing less than the presence of almighty God.

Elijah was ready and waiting to receive God's message because he refused to be entangled by the distractions around him. Of course, we can't ignore the legitimate demands of life. The goal of discernment is not to escape from the world but to keep one ear open for the voice of God amidst the noisiness of life.

Frankly, we notice what we care about and we hear what we love. I learned this like never before when my first daughter was born. I was amazed to discover I could pick out her voice from among a dozen other crying babies. From among a gang of kids hollering and squealing in the next room, a single yelp of pain from Bethany would bring me to my feet. This isn't so remarkable. Most parents practice this kind of discernment; we possess something like Daredevil's radar sense when it comes to our children. But we all pay attention to the things we care about. We are alert to the things and people we love. If you doubt this, drop a quarter on a crowded city sidewalk and watch the heads jerk around at the clink of the coin.

Loving God helps us pay attention to God. Worshiping God trains us to focus on God. In a thirteenth-century prayer that later became a popular song, Richard of Chichester offers to God his longing to "know thee more clearly, love thee more dearly, and follow thee more nearly." Our ability to know God clearly in the daily world is connected to loving God dearly.

There's no trick to paying attention to God, but certainly there are tools that sharpen this ability. One is prayer, something God's people have always practiced to keep in touch with God. When Solomon was about to be crowned as king over Israel, God came to him in a vision and invited the young man to ask for whatever he desired. Solomon prayed for "a discerning heart," and God honored that prayer. Like Solomon, those who want to experience God's presence will pray for discernment. In fact, the very act of prayer tunes our ears to listen for God. The more time we spend in conversation with God, the more adept we become at recognizing God's voice in other circumstances.

Each of my daughters practices discernments that elude me. Rachel is a photographer. She continually sees potential photos. As we walked together in the woods one autumn day, a discarded commode and rusty water heater caught Rachel's eye. All I saw was ugly trash, but Rachel circled the garbage snapping photos. I kidded her about her "trashy" photography until that photograph won a blue ribbon. Rachel has spent so much time snapping and studying photographs that she sees pictures I can't.

My other daughter, Bethany, is a musician who can discern subtleties of arrangement and composition to which I am deaf. So much time playing, singing, and listening to music has sensitized her hearing beyond the casual listener's.

By the same token, the more time we spend in prayer, the more we become sensitized to God's voice. The person who is disciplined in prayer may well hear God when others cannot.

Along with prayer, the study of Scripture is a crucial discipline of discernment all Christians recognize. Immersing ourselves in the Bible is the surest way to understand who God is. As we read of God's mighty acts and ponder God's messages delivered through prophets and letter-writers, we develop a "working knowledge" of the nature and character of God.

After reading comic books for so many years, I can often glance at a page and name the artist. Sometimes I can name the penciller as well as the artist who inked the finished product. The explosive dynamism of Jack Kirby is unmistakable, as are the commercial slickness of Neal Adams, the somber moodiness of Bernie Wrightson, and the expressive brushwork of Will Eisner. If I see a new movie poster by Frank Frazetta, I don't need to look for his signature. Frazetta's style is the giveaway. If I know the artist well enough, I can recognize his work.

The study of the Bible educates us in God's "style." The more familiar we become with God's workings in biblical times, the more likely we are to recognize God's handiwork in our own times and lives. If I live through a whole day and never once discern the presence of God, does that mean God was entirely absent from my life that day? Or does it mean I haven't gotten the hang of recognizing God's style?

Remember the lines we quoted earlier from Paul, the apostle's prayer for Christians to discern what truly comes from God. Having a scriptural knowledge of God's character helps us tell the difference between what comes from God and what does not. This is an important skill because false voices will often claim to speak for God.

Every so often a counterfeit comic book comes along and a few unwary people pay an exorbitant price for a worthless book. For instance, phony copies of *Eerie* #1 made the rounds a few years ago, and they sold quite well until the word got around. When DC reprinted the extremely rare *Action* #1, the company made the reprint an oversized edition and added an outer cover identifying the book as a facsimile. Even with these precautions, some unscrupulous sellers removed the extra cover and sold the mutilated reprint for huge sums of money.

The unfortunates who buy these bogus books usually don't know much about comics to start with. They will fall for a fake because they've never seen the real thing. At a convention I saw a well-meaning fan approach Dave Sim, the creator of *Cerebus the Aardvark*, with a bootleg copy of the first issue. Since I own the original, I recognized the fake, but the proud owner didn't. He presented the book to Dave Sim and asked him to sign it. Sim matter-of-factly opened the book and signed the name of fantasy artist Frank Frazetta at the bottom of the first page.

The bewildered fan looked at the signature and sputtered, "But you aren't Frank Frazetta!"

"And that's not *Cerebus* #1," Sim said, and he proceeded to point out the telltale signs that the book was a fake.

The surest defense against being led astray by phony gods is firsthand knowledge of the one-and-only true God. Fakes are easy to spot when you know the real thing. Faithful prayer and the study of Scripture are our best tools for a reliable knowledge of God.

Belonging to a community of faith helps too. "Who can discern his errors?" asks the psalmist (Ps. 19:12). Few of us are quick to recognize our own mistakes. God can and does speak to us through the counsel of spiritual friends.

One of the funniest stories in the Bible is the account of Balaam, a prophet who set out on a mission opposed to God's will. You'd think a prophet would see God's purposes clearly, but not Balaam. Somehow Balaam had convinced himself that he had God's permission to travel to Moab in order to pronounce a curse on Israel.

As Balaam rides his donkey toward Moab, an angel appears in the road with sword drawn to strike Balaam for his disobedience. The angel is invisible to Balaam, but Balaam's donkey can see the avenging spirit. To save his master's life, the donkey bypasses the angel by detouring into the field. The donkey's meandering enrages Balaam, and he beats the poor beast until she returns to the road.

Twice more the donkey rescues Balaam from the angel, and twice more the furious prophet beats his donkey. On the third occasion, God opens the donkey's mouth, and the beast asks Balaam why he is beating her.

In his rage, Balaam doesn't even notice the strangeness of the situation. He tells the donkey that if he had a sword in his hand, he would kill her on the spot. The donkey reminds Balaam of her consistent past good behavior, and then God allows Balaam to see the angel. The angel tells Balaam, "The donkey saw me and turned away from me these three times. If she had not turned away, I would certainly have killed you by now, but I would have spared her" (Num. 22:33). Balaam could have saved himself a great deal of danger, not to mention embarrassment, had he allowed his donkey to guide him on the way.

Sometimes others see clearly the things we cannot see for ourselves. On occasion God speaks through the voice of someone we love and trust. Before we disdain the advice of Christian friends, we do well to remember the humbling truth: If God can speak through a donkey, then God can speak through anyone.

The more we practice listening and watching for God, the better we become at recognizing God's presence. The letter to the Hebrews speaks of mature Christians "who because of practice have their senses trained to discern good and evil" (Heb. 5:14 NASB). As with so many skills, the best way to grow in discernment is to practice. Just making the commitment to pay attention to God will improve our sense of God's movement in the world. We will begin to see God sightings that others overlook. Countless people must have looked into the night skies two thousand years ago, but only three sages from the East saw God's plan revealed there. Because they were paying attention, the wise men were in place to welcome the Messiah while others who lived much nearer missed the event altogether.

## Following the Heart

Daredevil is the perfect model for discernment. He senses the world in its fullness, including the hidden world most people overlook. He weighs matters, judges what is important, and acts accordingly. Taking action is important. Daredevil is no curiosity-seeking eavesdropper; he scans the city buzz so that he will know where his help is needed.

When we discern God's will and do not act, we dull our senses. If we ignore God's promptings often enough, we forfeit our ability to sense those divine nudges. Jesus said that the one who hears his words "and acts on them" is like a man whose house is built on a solid foundation. The one who hears "and does not act" is like a man whose tottering house falls down in the storm (Luke 6:47–49 NRSV). Discernment is a waste of time if it doesn't determine our priorities and shape our decisions.

Matt Murdock lives and works in Hell's Kitchen, having returned to the part of town he grew up in. As a lawyer Matt has better options, but he operates a storefront law office specializing in pro bono work and service to the neighborhood. The comic book version of Hell's Kitchen festers with crime, poverty, drugs, and despair, dark streets where life is cheap and hope is in short supply.

Why does Daredevil hang out in Hell's Kitchen? His father died here. Others will die too, but maybe he can save a few. His gifts are great, and so are the needs of this place. Matt Murdock grew up Irish Catholic. He is scarcely a churchgoer, but his childhood faith has never died. Matt Murdock is in Hell's Kitchen because the people here need him. Daredevil stalks these dark tenements because he cannot ignore his calling.

Daredevil hears, smells, and feels the world more keenly than anyone else alive, but his super senses are not what have brought him to Hell's Kitchen. Superhuman radar doesn't keep him in these squalid streets. Daredevil finds his rightful path in the same way as the rest of us—by looking through the eyes of the heart.

# 10   X-Men
# In the World but Not of It

I n 1963 Marvel giants Stan Lee and Jack Kirby created a new comic book series about a bunch of outsiders who never fit in: mutants, the children of the atomic age and legacy of the Cold War. These children were born with, shall we say, "differences" to parents genetically damaged by exposure to atmospheric radiation. Lee wanted to call the book *The Mutants*, but his publisher felt young readers wouldn't recognize the word. So Lee compromised and dubbed the new title *X-Men*.

In the comic book version of genetic mutation, the mutant children invariably gain superhuman abilities, often at the cost of some physical oddity that sets them apart from others. Even when mutants exhibit no outward signs of difference, their extra-human powers evoke the envy and fear of ordinary people. The recurring theme in *X-Men* is alienation, the plight of people who are too different to fit in comfortably with the crowd. In the decade of bell-bottoms, troll dolls, and smiley faces, the X-Men eschewed standard superhero fare and offered an unexpectedly somber study in discrimination.

Almost from the beginning the series was overshadowed by more popular books devoted to Spider-Man, the Fantastic Four, Thor, Iron Man, and the Avengers. So to improve sales the writers and editors tried several ploys: introducing new costumes, killing the team leader, and breaking the group into individuals or pairs in separate adventures. Even outstanding artists like Jim Steranko and Neal Adams offered their skills to the flagging title. Nothing worked.

In view of the book's dark tone, perhaps the series' ongoing struggle is not surprising. Could the world really make a place for these children of the bomb? Could those mutant youngsters with unnatural gifts find a place alongside "normal" people?

Apparently not. After issue #66, *X-Men* ceased publication. A seven-year performance may be respectable for a modern comic book, but it was disappointing in 1970. By comparison, *Avengers* debuted the same month as *X-Men* and has continued without interruption for more than forty years.

Comic book characters rarely rest in peace. In 1975 a fresh creative team revived the X-Men team with a new international cast including Storm, Nightcrawler, and Wolverine. The latter soon became the most popular member of the team. The scrappy Wolverine was the ultimate outsider, set apart from humans by his mutant powers, isolated from his teammates by his savagery, and alienated even from himself. His mysterious origins and inner conflict fascinated readers, and his adamantium claws made him the darling of action fans.

Thanks to vivid characters and a strong creative team, the new *X-Men* book was a runaway hit, one of the most remarkable success stories since *Superman*. In the last quarter of the twentieth century, *X-Men* and its many spin-off titles were the hottest property in town. When *X-Men* rebooted and renumbered in 1991 with a brand-new first issue, sales reached a record-smashing eight million copies, the best-selling single issue in comic-book history.

The mythology of the X-Men universe is simple. Normal human beings belong to the species *Homo sapiens*. Mutants represent the rise of a new species, *Homo superior*. Mutants have gifts that set them apart from others. The world at large resents mutant powers and fears the traits that make *Homo superior* different. This tension is the heart of the series.

In X-Men stories, frightened humanity expresses its escalating distrust in myriad ways. Mobs attack mutants who publicly display their powers. The U.S. Senate debates a mutant registration act. Monstrous robotic Sentinels scour the world on a mutant-extinction mission. In the nation of Genosha, mutants are tattooed, numbered, and sent to forced labor. Tales set in a hypothetical future envision mutant concentration camps.

Being a mutant is a gift carrying a heavy cost. Threading through years of individual stories is a larger saga about how mutants find different strategies for coming to terms with society. Mutants exist in this world, yet they exist apart from the prevailing culture. The mutant population must confront one fundamental and inescapable reality: mutants are in the world, but they are not of the world.

Do those words sound familiar?

## A World of Difference

Throughout history the church of Jesus Christ has often described Christian experience in precisely the same manner: Christians are in the world but not of it. I experience what this struggle means when I travel outside my own country, which I love to do. I enjoy immersing myself in a different culture where everything is foreign to me, from the language, food, and customs to the music and even TV programs. Especially intriguing to me are the subtle differences involving eye contact, body language, personal space, and social etiquette.

Of course, being a stranger in a strange land has its disadvantages. I've accidentally offended locals because I didn't know what was expected. On the other hand, locals have occasionally taken advantage of my naiveté or ineptness with strange money; in a country where I don't speak the language, I experience the helplessness of instant illiteracy. After a couple of weeks of exotic meals, I usually long for a hamburger.

Even well-meaning folks may underline how far away from home I am. On a recent trip abroad, whenever I mentioned I was from Kentucky, I was met by the same response: "Yes! Fried chicken!" I appreciated the attempt to make a connection, but every repetition of that conversation reminded me that I was among people who didn't know me and didn't understand where I came from.

The New Testament describes Christian faith in a similar way—like a lifelong visit to a foreign land. Unquestionably we're in this world along with everybody else hurtling through space on planet Earth. Yet in some sense we don't belong to this world. We're foreigners far from our true home, outsiders frequently reminded that we don't fit in here.

Paul captures the longing of many Christians and the sense of being out of place when he writes, "But our citizenship is in heaven. And we eagerly await a Savior from there, the Lord Jesus Christ" (Phil. 3:20).

Our citizenship is in heaven! The church should issue a green card to the newly baptized, because Christians are

137

definitely resident aliens. We don't set our hopes on anything in this world, nor conduct ourselves according to the rules of this world. To be a Christian is a little like stepping out of a canoe onto the shore. We're on the way to our permanent home, but for the moment we have one foot in each world, balanced precariously between living in the present and belonging to a world that awaits our future homecoming.

Jesus never sugarcoated this tension. He spoke bluntly to his disciples about living in the world and following a savior that the world rejects. On the night before his crucifixion, he told his friends, "If you belonged to the world, it would love you as its own. As it is, you do not belong to the world, but I have chosen you out of the world. That is why the world hates you" (John 15:19).

Consider the experience of the first Christians. When Rome burned in AD 64, Nero needed a scapegoat to blame for the fire. He chose the Christians. In punishment for their imaginary crimes, Nero attacked the church with gleeful viciousness. Some Christians were crucified; others were wrapped in animal skins and thrown to packs of wild dogs as public entertainment; still others were doused in oil and set afire at night so Nero could drive his chariot through the royal gardens by the light of burning Christians. The Roman public was willing to play along with Nero's monstrous sport because dislike of Christians was widespread even before official persecution began.

How did Christians earn such enmity from their neighbors? Let us count the ways:

1. In a time of religious pluralism, Christians were branded as small-minded and judgmental because they rejected the vast array of gods worshiped in the Roman culture and insisted theirs was the only true God.

2. Christians practiced a morality that infuriated some and embarrassed others: Believers shunned drunkenness and gluttony, refused to leave unwanted infants to die in the woods, upheld that a healthy sexuality remained within the marriage covenant, treated slaves humanely and with compassion, and avoided the gladiatorial "games" where criminals, slaves, and prisoners of war died for the amusement of cheering crowds.

3. Followers of Jesus were deemed political subversives because they refused to worship the Roman leader Caesar as the embodied spirit of the goddess Roma.

In short, Christians found themselves in the Roman Empire but not of the Roman Empire. The first believers were either unwilling or unable to participate fully in the culture that surrounded them. They were in Rome but could not do as the Romans. For the crime of being different from others, Christians earned the contempt of their communities and the wrath of the government. As Jesus had predicted, loving the Lord invited the world's hatred.

The situation for Christians hasn't entirely changed over the centuries. In many parts of the world confessing Jesus is still a dangerous act. A church in Egypt was granted government permission to demolish and rebuild their building, but after the demolition was complete the permit to rebuild was revoked. Before a U.N. Commission on Human Rights, Chinese citizens testified to beatings, imprisonment, and torture aimed at Christians in their homeland, but for the eleventh year in a row the Commission voted not to censure China for human rights abuse. When my daughter joined a group of Christian students traveling to South America to work in an orphanage, she was warned not to mention any intention of sharing her faith lest her visa request be denied.

Even in democratic countries the prevailing culture may be antagonistic to Christianity. For instance, the ridiculous Ned Flanders in *The Simpsons* represents the norm for portraying Christians on television and in the movies. Community athletic teams increasingly schedule events on Sunday, forcing youth to choose between beloved activities and worship. A recent review of American history textbooks suggested that positive references to Christianity had been systematically eliminated. A student in one of my university classes complained that her anthropology professor had labeled the Genesis creation stories as "mythic garbage."

Beyond a growing disapproval specifically aimed at Christianity, we must also take into account the widening gulf between Christian moral and ethical values and the loosening norms of the larger culture—behavior that leaves Christians out of step with others. When the movie *Batman* came out in 1989, I recall complaining to a friend that I wouldn't take my children to see it because the caped hero hops into bed with his girlfriend. My friend, who was living with his significant other at the time, was appalled by my "closed-minded attitude." Increasingly, Christian perspectives on morality are simply incomprehensible to many.

Jesus's prayer for God to protect his disciples is as timely today as twenty centuries ago: "I have given them your word and the world has hated them, for they are not of the world any more than I am of the world" (John 17:14).

Welcome, Christians, to the ranks of the misunderstood and the despised—the fellowship of those who are always in the world but never of the world.

Welcome to the church.

Welcome to the X-Men.

# Living with Dual Citizenship

The heroic team of mistrusted mutants provides uncanny parallels for Christians attempting to cope with a world to which we do not belong. Like the church itself, Marvel's misfit mutants don't always agree on the best strategy for being in the world but not of it. Overall, the mutants in *X-Men* books explore four different ways of relating to the world—approaches the church has sometimes adopted too:

- peacefully coexisting with the world
- attacking the world
- compromising to fit into the world
- withdrawing from the world

Although wheelchair bound, Charles Xavier, or Professor X, the founder of the X-Men, possesses the most gifted mutant brain on the planet. With his formidable psychic abilities, Xavier could exercise immense power over mere *Homo sapiens*. For a mind reader and telepath, the possibilities for blackmail, extortion, and coercion are almost endless. Xavier could easily set himself up as the secret power behind the world's leaders; with little risk or exertion he could mentally rule the world while remaining safely ensconced behind the walls of his upstate New York mansion.

But Professor X has a different vision. He dreams of the day when humans and mutants can live beside one another in acceptance and mutual respect. To this end he's established his school for mutants and gathered the original X-Men. Xavier's first class of mutants consisted of five teenagers with diverse powers. Scott Summers was the taciturn second-in-command with the code

141

name Cyclops because of the destructive beams emanating from his eyes. Rich boy Warren Worthington III was the winged Angel. Bobby Drake, the Ice Man, could generate freezing temperatures and sheathe his body in ice. Hank McCoy, whose abnormally large hands and feet gave him superhuman agility, called himself the Beast. The last student to join the team was Jean Grey, or Marvel Girl, a young woman who could move objects by sheer mental power.

Xavier recruited these remarkable teenagers so he could instill in them his philosophy of using mutant powers for the betterment and protection of humankind. Commentator Peter Sanderson describes the role of mutantkind—or *Homo superior*—in this way: "It was like the religious idea of the Elect, a specially blessed segment of humanity destined for greater things than the rest. . . . Charles Xavier taught his students to use their abilities to benefit humanity, even if the rest of humanity hated and distrusted them; Xavier was preaching the superhero genre's version of Christ's precept to turn the other cheek."[1]

Jesus understandably comes to mind when you consider Professor X gathering disciples around him in hopes of creating a better world. His vision is not so unlike the Christian's: to unite a world where the strong defend the weak, unique powers are used for the common good, and differences are not only tolerated but celebrated—and channeled for a higher purpose.

## Out of or Into the World?

In the strictest sense, the X-Men were never superheroes. They had superpowers and were unquestionably heroic, but they didn't embark on a general mission of righting wrongs and working for justice at large. Their calling was

142

more specific. Xavier created the X-Men to foster better relations between mutants and normal people—to be agents of social change.

In practice, this usually meant battling the machinations of evil mutants who didn't share Xavier's dream. (What's a comic book without battles and villains, after all?) These mutant foes might be petty bank robbers who misused their powers for a quick buck or other adversaries driven by a dream in competition with Xavier's.

One such idealistic enemy is Magneto. Complex villains are more satisfying than the two-dimensional variety, and Magneto is a complicated bundle of idealism, pragmatism, and contradictions. Magneto appeared in the first issue of *X-Men* and remains a persistent thorn in Xavier's side to this day. Erik Magnus Lehnsherr, aka Magneto, was never a petty thug with superpowers. His schemes were grandiose and his motives unclear.

Eventually readers learn that Lehnsherr had been imprisoned as a child in the Auschwitz concentration camp, where his gypsy family died, but he bitterly survived. After his magnetic powers awakened, Magneto became convinced that mutants were bound to suffer the same fate as the unfortunate inmates of the Nazi death camps. Resolving to stop that persecution, Magneto declared war on the human race.

Xavier and Magneto had once been close friends, but their clashing ideologies turned them into enemies. Magneto's philosophy is simple. Humanity has repeatedly proved its suspicion and persecution of those who are different. *Homo superior* cannot live peaceably with *Homo sapiens*. One race must overcome the other. Magneto is resolved that his side will prevail.

Charles Xavier and Magneto represent two extreme ideas about how mutants might deal with humankind.

Between those opposite poles, other mutants have chosen other possibilities. Many mutants have sought to fit into the world in spite of their differences.

For instance, a mutant named Polaris dyed her green hair a more natural shade so she could pass for a human.

A mutant with the ability to generate displays of light took the stage name Dazzler and used her powers to gain an appreciative audience for her music performances. Dazzler let her fans assume the light show was artificially projected, but when the public found Dazzler was a mutant, her career crashed.

The X-Man Angel kept his wings a secret when they sprouted during puberty. Whenever Warren was in public, he wore an uncomfortable harness under his clothing to crush his wings and hide them from sight.

Some mutants have such non-human physical characteristics that disguising themselves as normal people is nearly impossible. One such mutant is the second generation X-Man Nightcrawler. With dark blue fur, yellow eyes, pointy ears, three-fingered hands, and a tail, Nightcrawler could never pass himself off as a human being—at least not until Tony Stark invented the image inducer, a pocket-sized device that projects a hologram allowing Nightcrawler to cloak himself in a human image.

The problem with "passing" for human is that the mutant must deny his or her true nature. This particular compromise never lasts long. Either the secret gets out or the mutant tires of the pretense. Angel, for instance, eventually renounced his secret identity so he would never again have to hide his wings. Nightcrawler abandoned the image inducer after only a few months, deciding it was better to be himself in public without shame or deception.

The fourth strategy adopted by some mutants is a retreat from the world. If humanity hates us, they reason, we'll drop out of sight. We have no hope of setting things right in this messed up world, so we'll pull out entirely.

Among mutants, the Morlocks represent the most extreme example of withdrawing from the world. This community of mutants, many of them misshapen and abused, made a home in abandoned tunnels beneath New York City. Hidden from the eyes of the world, the Morlocks lived in peace and built their own separate culture in the damp darkness. Eventually their hiding place was uncovered and a group called the Marauders attacked. Many of the hidden mutants were massacred. Those who did survive withdrew still further from the world, seeking refuge in an alien dimension.

Can you see parallels between the four strategies used by Marvel's mutants and the differing ways Christians deal with the world?

Sometimes we Christians are so intimidated by the opinions or prejudices of others that we find it easier to keep a tactful silence about our own beliefs. We don't actually deny our faith, but by our silence we pass as people without Christian conviction or identity.

Or maybe we retreat from a culture that offends us. Monasticism is withdrawal in its purest form, but modern Christians find many other ways to withdraw from a culture whose values offend us, such as pulling our children out of public school or forbidding cable television in our house.

Magneto's decision to make war on the culture may seem outlandish to us, but many Christian circles cultivate an attitude of us-versus-them. This worldview lies behind many Christian political action groups, boycotts of companies with harmful policies, and picketing a theater where an offensive movie is showing.

Charles Xavier's dream of service and peaceful acceptance is an attractive vision for many Christians. Every

145

time Christians help "outsiders," we pursue peace for all. Soup kitchens, refugee adoption programs, jail visitations, and special offerings for the family who lost their home to a fire are typical ways Christians serve and love the world in the name of Christ.

Which of these represents the most faithful way to be a Christian in the world but not of the world? I couldn't answer that for anyone but myself. Far be it from me to pass judgment on someone else's manner of following Jesus. Frankly, I see both strengths and drawbacks in each of these approaches.

Withdrawal protects our own holiness, and quiet compromise keeps the peace. But in either case we deprive the world of our witness. Jesus clearly calls us out of the world to follow him, but Jesus also sends us into the world bearing his love. No matter how we live out our faith, we must answer both callings with equal fervor.

Battling the world may be the best way of building a more just and healthy society, but such an approach easily turns into a judgmental and arrogant attitude that is far from the spirit of Jesus. Making enemies is easy enough; loving them is considerably harder.

Even Xavier's approach of loving service has a serious shortcoming. After all, Professor X is content with tolerance. He doesn't try to make converts. How could he? Mutants are born; one can't simply join the club. But mere coexistence falls short of Christianity's calling. The church actively seeks to bring outsiders into the family.

## Bridging Far-Flung Worlds

Comic fans love crossovers, meetings between characters from different books. For instance, the Avengers crossed over into X-Men #9. For their part, the X-Men guest starred in *Fantastic Four* #28 and *Avengers* #53. Intra-company superhero encounters were a staple at Marvel in their early days. Crossovers remain commonplace in most comic books, a guarantee of increased sales.

Far rarer are crossovers between characters from different companies. Once upon a time, DC was DC, Marvel was Marvel, and never the twain did meet. Then in 1976 DC and Marvel jointly released the oversized *Superman vs. The Amazing Spider-Man*. That landmark event brought together the flagship characters from each company and opened the way for future inter-company crossovers. Since such stories raise questions of top billing, copyright, and fair treatment of all characters as well as requiring writers, artists, and editors approved by both companies, these crossovers are still relatively infrequent. For instance, the Avengers and Justice League of America crossover was discussed for nearly twenty years before the first issue finally hit the stands.

The X-Men have also had the opportunity to meet characters across the great divide of publishing boundaries. Marvel's X-Men and DC's Teen Titans clashed in a story with almost too many characters to track. An even stranger crossover brought *X-Men* into the *Star Trek* universe, where the mutant band came face-to-face with the crew of the USS *Enterprise*. Readers scarcely knew what to make of such an unlikely pairing of distinctly different casts.

The *X-Men/Star Trek* encounter underscores why fans enjoy these comics so much. Crossovers between different companies actually represent a meeting between entirely different universes. These stories mark the intersection of worlds that have never touched. Characters have their eyes opened to people and realities of which they've never dreamed. The more different these worlds are, the more energy arises when they "collide." Just imagine Superman meeting Archie and his pals in Riverdale!

147

The X-Men's encounters with characters from different realities offer a fifth way for Christians to think about our relationship with people outside the church: a genuine crossover between different worlds.

Too often the church waits for "outsiders" to enter our reality. We publish a worship schedule and unlock the doors, as if the multitudes will come flooding in. Or we try to guilt others into joining us, stressing what's wrong with them and what's right with us. In ways both formal and informal, we insist that outsiders become like us before we make room for them. The implicit message is clear: We won't set foot in your world; you'll have to meet us in our world.

Instead of these dead-end approaches, maybe we should cross over to the world others live in. This doesn't mean sacrificing our principles or compromising our integrity. In fact, an honest-to-goodness crossover requires being true to ourselves while according the same privilege to others. Unless we remain faithful to our calling, we have no story to share with others. On the other hand, unless we are willing to honestly listen to others, why should they listen to us? When different worlds meet, fresh possibilities arise. New relationships are forged. Doors swing open to mutual trust and sharing.

Commonplace in comic books is the inevitable battle that erupts upon the first meeting between characters from different worlds. Crossovers almost always begin with mis-understanding and conflict. We should not be surprised if our effort to meet people from another world begins in the same way. But beyond the initial friction is the possibility, even the likelihood, of friendship. Crossing over builds bridges, and bridges open a path into a new future.

Marvel's mutants reveal the thorny challenge of being in the world yet not of the world. Fearful mutants conceal

148

their identities and seek a compromise. The purists withdraw and live in retreat. Some mutants draw the battle lines, while others strive for the separate races to coexist in peace. These mutant strategies echo similar courses Christians often choose.

Personally, I prefer the fifth possibility. I believe God is rooting for a crossover. After all, isn't that what Jesus did? In the truest sense, Jesus crossed over from heaven to meet humanity where we live. He brought his world—the kingdom of God—into our world. Even after Jesus arrived on planet Earth, he continued to cross over. He crossed over social boundaries. He crossed over religious divisions. He crossed over the borders of economics, gender, race, morality, and politics. And he invited his disciples to follow in his footsteps. "As the Father has sent me," Jesus told his followers, "I am sending you" (John 20:21).

Writing of the centuries-old division between the Jewish world and the secular or "Gentile" world, Paul tells us those radically different realities have found a meeting place in Christ. Jesus "has destroyed the barrier, the dividing wall of hostility," so that he could "reconcile both of them to God through the cross" (Eph. 2:14, 16).

The sacrificial love of Jesus bridges far-flung worlds and connects every conceivable reality. That's the ultimate crossover.

# 11 The Fantastic Four

## The Ties That Bind

n the early 1960s, superheroes were beginning to recover from the collapse of costumed super-do-gooders that nearly wiped out those characters a decade earlier. The reasons for the decline of superheroes are complex, but by the mid-1950s Superman, Batman, and Wonder Woman were virtually the only remainders of DC's pantheon. In an effort to rejuvenate the field, DC Comics began to retool versions of earlier characters. Editor Julius Schwartz offered readers a new and improved Flash in 1956, and this first appearance of the new Flash is generally hailed as the beginning of the Silver Age of comics. These Silver Age heroes were the literary heirs of the Golden Age characters of the Depression and War years.

The Flash tryout in *Showcase* #4 generated sufficient enthusiasm to give the Scarlet Speedster his own book. A revamped Green Lantern followed in 1959, and the following year DC brought out the team book *Justice League of America*. Inspired by a similar Golden Age team, the Justice League was a surefire hit, bringing together heavy hitters like the Flash and Green Lantern with characters of lesser popularity like Wonder Woman, Martian Manhunter, and Aquaman. On occasion Superman and Batman also showed up. With so many characters between the same covers, *Justice League* had something for every superhero fan, and the book sold very well.

The success of the Justice League sparked interest in the offices of Marvel Comics. In its earlier incarnation as Timely Comics, Marvel had once been a contender in the superhero field with Golden Age greats like Captain America, the Human Torch, and the Sub-Mariner. Half-hearted efforts to revive some of those characters in the 1950s had fizzled, and Marvel was reduced to publishing monster and mystery comic books for younger readers. The superhero renaissance at DC prompted Marvel publisher Martin Goodman to get in on the act. Goodman asked longtime comic writer Stan Lee to come up with a superhero team for Marvel.

Disenchanted with Marvel's juvenile niche in the market, Lee decided to create the kind of characters he personally wanted to read about. With artist Jack Kirby, who'd been in the field even longer than Lee, the writer scripted the first issue of the *Fantastic Four*. In the early days of the book, Lee's writing was somewhat tentative, and Kirby's art scarcely hinted at the dazzling creativity he would later unleash. Yet from the very beginning, *Fantastic Four* established itself as a comic book determined to break the rules and conventions of the genre.

The Fantastic Four were superheroes such as no one had ever seen: four friends—former colleagues who gained their super-

powers as astronauts exposed to mysterious cosmic rays—
who divide their time between fighting cosmic menaces
and squabbling with each other.

The four are Johnny Storm (the Human Torch), who
bursts into flame; his sister Susan (the Invisible Girl),
who disappears; Reed Richards (Mr. Fantastic), whose
elastic limbs stretch unbelievably; and gruff pilot Ben
Grimm (the Thing), who turns into a monstrous figure of
tremendous strength. Here were characters with undeni-
ably distinct personalities and patterns of speech. Before
their origin, most superheroes had interchangeable personalities—powers and costumes differed, but practically
everyone talked alike, thought alike, and acted uniformly
kind and altruistic. Aside from sheer nobility, the older
superhero characters lacked convincing motivation for
their good deeds.

The disparate and rough-edged champions of the Fantastic Four departed radically from earlier cardboard
heroes. Each member of the foursome was a unique
character whose words and actions sprang convincingly
from their respective personalities. For example, the Thing
was chronically angry because he loathed his misshapen
appearance and Reed was overbearing because he was
uneasy with his own leadership. By the standards of that
time, these characters were deep, rich, and refreshingly
complex in motivation.

To further skew the usual patterns, these heroes groused,
bickered, and argued among themselves. This was definitely not how good guys behaved. An argument between
the Flash and Green Lantern? Out of the question. A tiff
between Superman and Batman? Unheard of! A meeting of
the Justice League degenerating into a brawl? Not before
Lee and Kirby's revolution, although later others began to
imitate their successful superhero style.

Until the Fantastic Four came along, superheroes were, with few exceptions, attractive, polite, and, well, heroic. Ben Grimm, aka the Thing, was none of those. Reminiscing about the qualities that set his Marvel team apart, Stan Lee writes, "Suffice it to say that the ever-lovin' Thing is bad-tempered, ill-mannered, crude, and not the most attractive guy you're apt to meet. Therefore, what could be more natural than that he would turn out to be the FF's most popular and beloved member!"[1]

Other eccentricities set the Fantastic Four apart. Instead of the typical romance endlessly frustrated by misunderstandings and secret identities, Susan Storm and Reed Richards were already engaged when the series began. As for secret identities, the Fantastic Four again broke the mold. From the beginning their identities were known to the world.

When Reed and Sue married in *Fantastic Four Annual* #3, the book again plowed new ground. Superhero marriages are not uncommon today. Even that perennial bachelor Superman tied the knot with Lois a few years ago. Yet the wedding of Mr. Fantastic and the Invisible Girl was a first. The Fantastic Four continued to push the envelope when Susan Richards gave birth to her son Franklin in *Fantastic Four Annual* #6.

Family ties are crucial to the Fantastic Four. In the first issue a complicated web of relationships was already sketched out. Susan (the Invisible Girl) is the older sister and surrogate mother for teenager Johnny (the Human Torch). Reed Richards (Mr. Fantastic) is engaged to Susan and also serves as a father figure to Johnny. Reed and Ben Grimm (the Thing) are almost like brothers. Their often-bumpy friendship stretches back to their roommate days in college. To add a tasty dash of soap-opera spice, Ben is a failed suitor for Susan's hand and resents her affections for Reed.

153

So after cosmic radiation gives them superpowers, the four friends set up housekeeping together in the Baxter Building, where they divide their time between fighting cosmic menaces and squabbling with each other. Along the way they wrestle with the common stuff of family life: paying the rent, transportation, jealousy, sharing chores, defining individual roles, hurt feelings, and finding reliable childcare.

What Stan Lee created was not so much a superhero team as a complicated family whose members just happen to have special abilities.

## The Motley Crew

If the X-Men offer us a view of the church in relationship with the world, the Fantastic Four give a picture of the church from within. The story of Reed, Susan, Ben, and Johnny is a parable of the church as a family of imperfect persons brought together by grace and held together by love.

Consider, for instance, how the Fantastic Four is made of all kinds of people. Like the church, this super foursome is a microcosm of diversity: Susan Storm Richards has a superpower that allows her to disappear—essentially, to fade into the background. She moves unnoticed and uncredited among other people. She's gentle and loving, but her gifts of nurturing are easily taken for granted. The female member of the Fantastic Four represents the overlooked and unappreciated people in the world. Sue demonstrates her underrated status when she elects to call herself the Invisible Girl.

Reed Richards is Sue's opposite, a born leader in the center of the action. He takes personal responsibility for the success of the team and the safety of his partners.

When things go wrong, Reed blames himself. His elastic body seemingly allows him to be everywhere at once, but his stretchability also suggests that he's pulled in conflicting directions. Reed wrestles with a demon he can never exorcise—the demon of failure. He lives in continual expectation of the next world-threatening menace. What if the leader of the Fantastic Four is unprepared for the next assault by Galactus? What if the Skrull invasion scheme catches him off guard? What if Mr. Fantastic's latest world-saving gadget sputters and misfires at the critical moment? What if the universe comes crashing down because Reed Richards stumbled?

A standing joke developed among longtime readers of the *Fantastic Four*. We came to anticipate the recurring scene in which Reed surveys some approaching menace while Sue stands to the side, one hand covering her mouth in apprehension, thinking, "I've never seen Reed so pensive, so grim!"

Reed Richards is not only haunted by the fear of future failure, he also torments himself remembering past failures. Specifically, Reed cannot make peace with the accident that created the Fantastic Four and transformed Ben Grimm into a monster. The Thing's presence is a constant reminder of Reed's blunder on the rocket and his ongoing failure to reverse the effects of the cosmic radiation.

Johnny Storm is the stereotypical teenager: hotheaded, always feeling like an outsider, rarely fitting in. His romances go awry. As the youngest member of the Fantastic Four, he sees himself as the odd man out. As the Human Torch, his flaming powers are a metaphor for the person who is afraid to let others draw near. Ironically, Johnny eventually hooks up with the ultimate outsider. Johnny marries a Skrull, a female of a shape-shifting alien race

155

from outer space. Johnny Storm is the archetype of all the people who long for intimacy and community but feel unable to bridge their separation.

Ben Grimm is the most troubled yet also the most compelling member of the Fantastic Four. Cosmic radiation gave Ben immense strength, but in exchange for power he must accept a grotesque appearance. Seconds after Ben changes into his orange, rocky form, Susan gasps that he has turned into "some sort of a thing." Ben bitterly adopts Sue's outburst of horror as his new name. His initial public appearances inspired terror, and normal people fled from the Thing. As a result, the Thing often wore an overcoat, sunglasses, and a low-brimmed hat. When Sue designed costumes for the team, the Thing was the only member to receive a helmet that hid his features. Simply put, Ben Grimm despises himself. He feels utterly unworthy of love and therefore is angry at the world.

What a motley crew! Most super teams are categorized by the powers they exhibit, but a catalogue of hang-ups better describes the Fantastic Four: inadequacy, inner conflict, guilt, alienation, loneliness, and self-loathing. Yet for all their foibles, these flawed people find a family in the Fantastic Four. They often bump and bruise one another, but along the way they also learn to take care of each other. Each person brings his or her needs into the family, and those needs are honored.

## See How They Love Each Other

We cannot expect any family to solve every problem for every member, but love looks for a way to heal and nurture. This principle is ever at work within the Fantastic Four.

Johnny Storm gradually matures because he discovers he can be himself within the dependable safety of his new family. His early days are characterized by rash decisions. The Human Torch is constantly flying off on some ill-considered mission that turns out to be too much for him as his fire weakens or a villain douses his flames. Yet even when Johnny's power fails him, his family does not.

When the young hero topples from the sky, invariably his teammates wait to catch him either in the far-reaching arms of Mr. Fantastic, in the strong hands of the Thing, or in his sister's invisible force field. Perhaps Johnny's juvenile pranks and endless practical jokes are the teen's way of testing his family, reassuring himself that they'll still love him even when he's unlovable.

Susan Storm Richards also grows up in the loving embrace of this odd family. The team members accept and love Sue as she is, but they also challenge her to become more. Empowered by the respect and expectations of her partners, the Invisible Girl extends her abilities. At first Sue's only power is super hiding, but over time she comes into her own as a formidable and heroic figure. Her gifts turn out to be far more impressive than anyone had first guessed.

Susan is one of those people who love to love others. The Fantastic Four offers a place where Sue can express her love as a sister, a friend, a wife, and, eventually, a mother. In spite of the inevitable spats and hurt feelings, Sue knows that she can safely love these people without fearing rejection or betrayal. As the Invisible Girl comes into her own as a person and hero, she finally drops her old name and becomes the Invisible Woman, an apt outward sign of her inward growth.

Reed Richards has not entirely shaken off his too-serious outlook. He will never be the poster boy for emotional openness. However, over time the team leader has learned to relax a little. In spite of Reed's occasional miscalculations and blunders, the world is still spinning, thanks to partners who step in to share the load. Johnny and Ben's running feud brings a smile to Reed's face, though he rarely joins in the hijinks. Becoming a father has put Reed in touch with the joys of life, and Susan's persistent love brings him out of his intellectual shell. The bitter recriminations Ben Grimm once aimed at Reed have turned into good-natured needling. As the Thing has forgiven Reed Richards for the accident that deformed him, perhaps Reed is beginning to forgive himself. While Mr. Fantastic is the most gifted member of the group, one suspects that Reed Richards would have lived an emotionally barren life if not for his membership in this ragtag family.

Benjamin J. Grimm has also found a home in the Fantastic Four. Even before the disastrous rocket flight, Ben was an angry, bitter man. In his youth Ben saw his brother killed in gang warfare, and for a while the bitter young man became a gang leader himself. In a sense the cosmic radiation merely manifested outwardly the ugliness that already infected Ben Grimm inwardly. Although Reed has never been able to turn his friend back to normal, belonging to the Fantastic Four has been a transformative experience for Ben. Here is a family that accepts him in spite of his warts—both the inner and the outer varieties.

I've lost count of the number of times the Thing has flown into a rage and Reed Richards has wrapped his rubbery body around and around his old friend to keep him from doing damage he will regret. I've always suspected the Thing could easily break loose from Mr. Fantastic but secretly longs to be restrained. He wants to be hugged into submission by people who care about him regardless of his fury. Acceptance by his friends has allowed the Thing to accept himself.

Indeed, the Thing is the powerhouse of the group, and he takes pride in the strength that allows him to do his share. Who knows how that vast strength might have been misused if not for the influence of his friends? Both the Hulk and the Thing are staggeringly powerful, and both are monsters in the eyes of the world. Perhaps Ben Grimm's story turns out better than the Hulk's because he is not alone. The Thing belongs to a family.

In the New Testament the idea of family is the most persistent way of describing the church. The first believers called each other brother and sister, the sons and daughters of one heavenly Father. Baptism was rebirth into the family of Christ. Paul describes the church as the "household of God" and at other times shifts his point of view to picture the church as the "bride of Christ." The first worship services took place in homes and centered on gathering at the table.

Even more than these symbolic trappings, the early church behaved like a family. "All who believed were together and had all things in common; they would sell their possessions and goods and distribute the proceeds to all, as any had need. Day by day, as they spent much time together in the temple, they broke bread at home and ate their food with glad and generous hearts" (Acts 2:44–46 NRSV). One ancient commentator summed up his impressions of the church in a few words: "See how they love each other!"

159

## Strength in Numbers

The church has never been perfect, not even in its first generation, but at its best the church is a family whose arms are open to all, especially those shunned by the world—the poor, the overlooked, the guilt-ridden, the broken, and the misfits. Paul underlines the importance of welcome and family love when he writes, "Consider your own call, brothers and sisters: not many of you were wise by human standards, not many were powerful, not many were of noble birth. But God chose what is foolish in the world to shame the wise; God chose what is weak in the world to shame the strong; God chose what is low and despised in the world" (1 Cor. 1:26–28 NRSV).

When asked why he socialized with undesirables, Jesus answered, "Those who are well have no need of a physician, but those who are sick; I have come to call not the righteous but sinners to repentance" (Luke 5:31 NRSV).

Jesus envisioned the church as a hospital for those who want to get well. When Jesus invites a man or woman to follow him, he calls that person into a community of love, faith, and nurture. In the church Christians learn to give and accept care. "Above all, maintain constant love for one another, for love covers a multitude of sins. Be hospitable to one another without complaining. . . . serve one another with whatever gift each of you has received" (1 Peter 4:8–10 NRSV).

When the love of Christ flows into and through the people of Christ, the church becomes a transforming and redemptive community, a family where outsiders find a place and imperfect people grow toward their best selves. Nowhere in all the many *Fantastic Four* stories is this transformative power shown more clearly than in issue #51, a tale titled "This Man . . . This Monster!"

The story revolves around an anonymous scientist whom we will call Damon, a petty man consumed by envy and embittered by imagined injustices. Damon feels his scientific genius has been overshadowed by the accomplishments of Reed Richards, and he devises a scheme by which to destroy his rival. By guile and scientific wizardry, Damon transforms himself into an exact duplicate of the Thing while turning the Thing back into his human identity of Ben Grimm. Masquerading as the Thing, Damon makes his way to the Baxter Building and infiltrates the Fantastic Four's headquarters.

The impostor arrives just in time to assist Reed Richards in a life-and-death experiment. To safeguard Earth from alien invasion, Reed hopes to find the secret of faster-than-light travel. To that end, Reed will explore subspace, a mysterious realm between dimensions. A long steel cable is Reed's only safety line. He entrusts the cable to the strong hands of the ersatz Thing and launches himself into subspace.

To his dismay, Reed finds himself hurtling toward an explosive zone where all matter is destroyed. In vain he tugs on the safety line. Damon ignores the plea for help. This is his opportunity to remove his rival forever—but suddenly Damon has doubts. Reed's trust touches him, as does Sue's concern for the man she loves. Reed's willingness to face terrible danger for no personal reward confuses Damon. Just as the masquerader makes up his mind to reel his rival to safety, the cable snaps.

Sue tries to leap into the vortex after Reed, but Damon pushes her back. He grabs the disappearing cable and is drawn into subspace, where he catches up with Reed Richards as he stands astride an asteroid speeding toward destruction. Reed is heartbroken that the man he assumes to be his old friend will now die at his side. He clasps the hand of the impostor and thanks him for years of friendship. Profoundly moved by Reed's unselfish love, Damon grabs Reed and uses the Thing's stolen strength to hurl Reed toward the interdimensional portal that leads back to Earth.

As Reed streaks from sight, Damon waves farewell and says, "So long, Richards! I hope you make it! As for me, I'm not gonna feel sorry for myself! Not many men get a second chance—to make up for the rotten things they've done in their lifetime! I guess I'm luckier than most! I got that chance! For I finally learned—what it means to have—a friend!"[2]

In the end Damon's inward transformation is far more miraculous than his outward change in appearance. Just a brief exposure to this loving family turns his heart around. He releases his anger and seizes the opportunity to be a new person. As he rides the meteor toward fiery death, Damon is monstrous on the outside, but on the inside he is truly and fully human for the first time in his life. By God's grace the church offers precisely this gift to fallen and broken human beings. "Come as you are," says the church, "and become what you were meant to be."

The Fantastic Four are interesting because they are not "a closed shop." The close-knit foursome knows how to make room for others. Although Marvel can't change the cover title to *Fantastic Five* or *Fantastic Nine* on a monthly basis, the team has often enlarged or reconfigured. For various reasons stand-ins have sometimes appeared to keep the team intact during someone's absence or incapacitation. Johnny's one-time girlfriend Crystal, Medusa of the Inhumans, Power Man, and She-Hulk have each taken a turn on the team's formal roster.

Beyond these affiliate members, the Fantastic Four adopt an array of friends and allies into the family. Some-

162

times former enemies such as the Silver Surfer or the Sub-Mariner become allies. At other times newcomers like the Black Panther or the Inhumans find a place within the collective heart of the team. Non-super types are welcome too, such as Johnny's college buddy Wyatt Wingfoot or the babysitter Agatha Harkness.

Marvel's "first family" knows how to keep the circle unbroken while still expanding the boundaries. The Fantastic Four are a role model for church life. A healthy family—or a healthy congregation—has a clear sense of its own identity while remaining open to outsiders who want to become insiders. Functional families welcome new members through marriage and remarriage, birth, adoption, foster care, in-laws, and friendship. The church also keeps its heart and its doors open, not merely willing but eager to embrace new sisters and brothers in Christ.

## Existing for a Mission

If you've gotten the impression that *Fantastic Four* is a pulp-paper soap opera, think again. Stan Lee and Jack Kirby were masters at injecting the realism of family life into their stories, but against that down-to-earth backdrop the writer and artist created epic adventures. When the Fantastic Four's signal flare blazed in the sky, the members of this family rallied to action. Fantastic Four have never been self-absorbed. They can't afford to be. They have a mission that matters more than their personal lives. Their collective job is saving the world, and that they do. They save the world from invaders—space invaders, undersea invaders, subterranean invaders. They save the world from Galactus and assorted cosmic menaces. They save the world from Dr. Doom, Annihilus, and the Pyscho-Man.

In short, the Fantastic Four exist for a mission, and they never forget it.

The church has a mission too. We mistake the meaning of the church if we think it exists only for the sake of its own members. In fact, the church has an important task reaching well beyond its own comfort and safety.

Of course, the church on its own can't save anybody. The church is like a lighthouse whose beacon points the way to safe harbor. The church has no light except the light of Christ shining through us in a dark world. That is our mission: to shine with the light of our Lord and by that light to invite others to share the grace that has saved us.

Outsiders have criticized the church for fixating on internal debates, annual budgets, and building programs while ignoring the needs of lost and hurting people next door. Perhaps this is one of the reasons so many people are indifferent to the church. What if the Fantastic Four never left the Baxter Building? Who would keep reading if the mission of the team consisted of nothing more than maintenance—laundry, house cleaning, meal preparation, and occasional remodeling? Even the staunchest fan would lose interest if Reed, Sue, Ben, and Johnny did nothing but take care of one another.

When the household of Christ is ingrown and self-focused, the church forsakes its purpose. After all, the crew of a lighthouse doesn't maintain the light for their own pleasure; they keep the light shining for the sake of people in danger. The church nurtures its members, empowers their gifts, and encourages their growth so they'll be ready for the great mission. That's why Jesus founded the church. After all, the fate of a world hangs in the balance.

Belonging to a family is a precious gift. Every one of us is searching for a family that will love us as we are, help

164

us grow into our best selves, and challenge us to make a difference in the world. The Fantastic Four are one such family. The church is another. Admittedly, the Fantastic Four have better uniforms and cooler gadgets than the church, but baptism is so much easier than exposure to cosmic radiation.

# What Is God Like?

T he Punisher versus Green Arrow? As much as comic fans love a brawl between unlikely opponents, especially the rare crossover between characters from different companies, this particular match doesn't look promising.

The Punisher totes more firepower than an NRA convention, not to mention the grenades and Gerber Mark II Combat Knife, and he kills without remorse.

Green Arrow carries—yes, indeed—a bow and gimmicky arrows; the original Green Arrow was a fun-loving adventurer who never harmed a fly.

A battle between the Punisher and Green Arrow probably wouldn't last longer than one page—no, make that one panel. Yet this particular contest represents an ongoing disagreement in our culture over clashing pictures of God.

Sure enough, people have many different ways of thinking about

God, and not everyone who uses the name "God" has the same idea in mind.

Maybe that shouldn't be so surprising. God is so big that no single notion of him will ever capture the fullness of who he is. In fact, most thinking about God consists of comparisons. We compare God with something tangible that can be seen and understood. For instance, when we call God "Father" or "Shepherd" or "King," we are really saying that the unseen heavenly God has some things in common with visible, earthly parents, sheepherders, and rulers.

In some ways our thinking about God is like the story of the blind men, each of whom felt a different part of the elephant. As a result, one blind man decided an elephant is like a pillar. Another likened the elephant to a snake. Still others compared the elephant to a wall, a rope, or a spike. Who was right? All of them. And none. Each experienced one small part of the elephant, but none of them had the whole picture.

How easy to make the same mistake with God, to grab hold of one tiny truth about him and think there's no more to discover. There's a bigger picture, to be sure. While some pictures are clearer and truer than others, no picture of God is altogether adequate.

Since comic books are largely devoted to bigger-than-life superheroes, you'll find that some of the most prevalent—if not always most accurate—ways of thinking about God are represented in those colorful pages.

## The God Who Strikes

First, take a good look at the Punisher. Before becoming the Punisher, Frank Castle was a natural-born soldier with icy nerves and an unswerving sense of justice. As a U.S. Marine captain and a decorated veteran of the Vietnam War, Castle had received training in martial arts, hand-to-hand combat, marksmanship, and proficiency with a wide range of weapons. The soldier's orderly world fell apart when mobsters murdered his wife and two small children. From that moment, Castle devoted himself to a war on the home front, a war against organized crime.

Calling himself the Punisher, Castle donned a black battle suit with a skull emblazoned across his chest. He armed himself with heavy firepower and a new devotion to clean up the streets. His methods were ruthless and effective. Most comic book heroes either refuse to kill or else do so only under the most extreme duress. Not the Punisher. He considers himself the judge, jury, and executioner. His code of justice is simple: Those who live by the gun deserve to die by the gun.

In the first Punisher movie, when Frank Castle (played by Dolph Lundgren) is accused of having killed hundreds of people, he grunts, "It's a work in progress."[1]

Once a criminal is on the Punisher's list, his fate is decided. The technique may vary, but the results are certain. Whether shot, exploded, garroted, or thrown from the Empire State Building, evildoers receive their just deserts, and then the Punisher moves on to his next target. If so-called heroes like Spider-Man get in the way of Castle's holy crusade, the Punisher's gun plays no favorites. The Punisher is absolutely assured of his own righteousness. Anyone who opposes him is on the wrong side, and the wrong side of the Punisher is a dangerous place to be.

Is this how you think of God?

I've lost count of how many times I've sat beside a hospital bed or held the trembling hands of troubled souls confessing fear that God is punishing them for their wrongs. A rebellious child is the punishment for marital infidelity. Cancer is the payback for a long-ago abortion. Alcoholism is the penalty for a wild youth. All of these convictions are built upon the certainty that God loves to smack sinners, that he takes note every time we spit on the sidewalk, curse a rude driver, or harbor a lustful desire. On some celestial computer, this God tracks and tallies our transgressions, waiting for sufficient evidence to lower the boom. He's the Cosmic Punisher, hating sinners, ever-ready to hunt them down and strike them out.

That image doesn't work for me. I don't doubt our actions carry repercussions or that God is ultimately just, but I can't believe God sits around planning ways to get even with us for our mistakes. In fact, the Bible says God is slow to anger and quick to forgive; Jesus tells us God is like a loving father who welcomes home the runaway son who spent all his money on booze and prostitutes. Unlike the Punisher, God is quite fond of sinners, and when he hunts them down it's in order to bring them home.

## The God Who's Conflicted

If power is the primary requirement for divine status, then maybe Galactus fits the bill. The first appearance of the matchless Galactus, in *Fantastic Four* #48, still evokes a thrill for longtime comic fans. He was so huge that he made even the tallest, largest humans appear as mere gnats, and he wielded immeasurable power, sweeping away the Fantastic Four as a mere irritation.

You see, the Fantastic Four learned Galactus had come to Earth, guided by his faithful herald the Silver Surfer, to devour our world. As Galactus began to construct the

169

huge siphoning machines that would drain Earth of its elemental energies, however, the Silver Surfer became acquainted with an earthling named Alicia Masters. The Surfer was so moved by the young woman's beauty and gentleness that he tried to persuade Galactus to leave Earth intact and seek out some lifeless world to devour.

Galactus contemptuously rejected the proposal. To the Ravager of Worlds, the inhabitants of Earth were no more significant than the crawling swarms in an anthill. But in an anguish of conscience, the Silver Surfer turned against the lord he'd served for ages; in the end Galactus did leave Earth unscathed and grudgingly acknowledged a spark of worthiness in human beings.

Unfortunately, this Galactus and Silver Surfer image is often accepted as a true picture of God. I've heard well-meaning preachers explain that God was angry at us and Jesus offered himself on the cross to change God's mind. In this way of thinking, God dislikes us because we are sinful and annoying, but Jesus comes to our rescue and convinces God to have mercy on us.

This contradicts the most basic biblical teaching: God loves us, he has always loved us, and nothing we do can ever make him stop loving us.

Far from disdaining or despising humanity, God's heart aches for us to respond to the divine love. We mustn't think that Jesus came into the world with his own plan. God sent Jesus into the world in order to carry out God's plan for bringing sinners home. Jesus didn't die on the cross to change God's feelings about us. Jesus's sacrificial love is the perfect expression of God's feelings for us. However we interpret the reconciling work of the cross, we must begin by understanding that Jesus came because "God so loved the world" (John 3:16).

# The God Who's All-Seeing

Another popular image of God is represented by Uatu the Watcher, who has been observing the Marvel universe for many years, ever since *Fantastic Four* #13. As you might guess from his title, the Watcher's role in life is to watch. He belongs to an eons-old race whose home planet has been converted to one vast computer. The race of Watchers roams the universe observing the rise and fall of civilizations and amassing endless information for purposes known only to themselves. Their most sacred vow is non-involvement. They watch life unfold, but they do not interfere.

Uatu the Watcher is assigned to our corner of the universe and is usually present at times of crisis. Although he's pledged never to intervene in the affairs of others, the Watcher sometimes bends the rules when the stakes are high. For instance, when Galactus first came to Earth intending to drain the energies from our planet, the Watcher took a stand on the side of humanity. In spite of his vast powers, the Watcher didn't oppose Galactus directly. He tried a quieter, nonviolent tactic first—to hide our planet. When that ploy failed, Uatu informed the Fantastic Four of the one weapon that could thwart Galactus. Then the Watcher used his powers to guide the Human Torch to the home world of Galactus where the Ultimate Nullifier could be found and retrieved.

Fascinating, isn't he? With nearly unlimited power, the Watcher chooses not to involve himself in the dilemmas of others. Nevertheless, his heart is in the right place, and when truly crucial situations unfold, the Watcher is likely to give events a nudge in the proper direction.

This is precisely the kind of God many people want to believe in—a God who watches but doesn't get involved in daily life. A God like that doesn't intrude and doesn't demand much. Don't bother this God, and he won't bother you. Yet, like a safety net, he'll be there for emergencies, ready to bail you out of the big messes, like when the heart attack strikes or the car begins to skid on an icy highway. Call on the Watcher-God to swoop in and set things right; when the crisis passes, the Watcher-God will retreat to the heavens until needed again.

For people who vaguely believe in God but don't want to do much about it, the Watcher is a tidy option. But the problem with the Watcher is that most of us yearn for a God who will take care of us all of the time, not just some of the time. Besides, while the Watcher's certainly a kinder vision of God than the Punisher or Galactus, the usually aloof Watcher is no more biblical than his rivals.

Jesus says the Creator is wholeheartedly involved in the life of the creation: He laments the fall of a sparrow, counts every hair on your head, and holds your tears in his bottle. Indeed, the very coming of Jesus into the world reveals a hands-on God who refuses to remain at a distance.

## The God Who's Out There . . . Somewhere

Let's examine one last misleading image of God, this one represented by Odin, Lord of Asgard. In an earlier chapter we've already mentioned how Stan Lee adapted Norse mythology for the character of Thor. In the Thor comic book, Odin is the supreme big cheese, the absolute top cat. He rules over Asgard, the home of the Norse gods, and by implication he rules over Earth as well. Indeed, he calls himself the All-Father.

While Odin is almighty, for some reason he's never any help when the world really needs him. Sometimes his hands are tied by some cosmic prophecy. Other times he's off on a mysterious quest and no one can find him. Too often the universe is going to hell in a handbasket and Odin's simply not there.

In one of my favorite storylines, the end of the world is approaching, and only Odin can avert total destruction. Unfortunately, Odin is bedded down in the sacred Odin-Sleep, and no one is allowed to wake him.

Nothing could be further from the picture of God painted in the Bible. The God of Israel is a God strong to save, a God whose arm is long enough to reach anywhere. God never fails or forsakes us, never dozes off at the wheel.

Indeed, the psalmist assures us, "he who watches over you will not slumber" (Ps. 121:3). Unlike Odin, the real God is always there for us and can always provide what we need.

## The God Who Is Ready for Anything

Green Arrow gets my vote as the best image of God in the comic-book world. The adventurous archer offers a better way of thinking about God than does the avenging executioner.

Oh, I know many fans consider Green Arrow a silly superhero. One longtime reader of comics said to me, "Someday someone with nothing better to do will write a history of the goofiest comic book heroes ever created, and Green Arrow will get a whole chapter of his own."

DC Comics writers have revised Green Arrow over the years to make him more palatable. In the 1970s Green Arrow became "relevant" and confronted issues like racism, overpopulation, and pollution. Today's Green Arrow is a character both more serious and more realistic, at least as comic fans define realistic. There's scarcely a trick arrow in sight these days.

I've enjoyed all the incarnations of this latter-day Robin Hood, but my heart belongs to the original version of Green Arrow who made his first appearance in 1941. He and his sidekick Speedy rode around in the Arrowmobile or the Arrow Plane and took on criminals using a bow and a variety of gimmicky arrows.

Green Arrow and Speedy hung around for decades without becoming first-stringers. Their adventures were usually relegated to backup features, but those stories were great fun to read. No matter what dilemma faced the Emerald Archer, he would always pull out of his quiver just the right arrow for that occasion.

For instance, if a crook were about to get lost in the crowd, Green Arrow would keep the felon in sight with the Heli-Spotter Arrow, a sort of hovering mirror affair. A fleeing getaway car was easily followed with the Fountain Pen Arrow hooked to the bumper, leaving a trail of ink on the highway. A poison gas attack? No problem! Use the Fan Arrow to disperse the deadly fumes. Is a villain brandishing a lit stick of dynamite? The Rain Arrow will extinguish the fuse and save the day. The Net Arrow saw a lot of use, as did the Boomerang Arrow. Then there were Flare Arrows, Dry-Ice Arrows, Fire-Cracker Arrows, the Two-Stage Rocket Arrow, the Acetylene-Torch Arrow, the Aqua-Lung Arrow, and the rarely used but occasionally very helpful Fake-Uranium Arrow.

A Green Arrow story never generated much suspense. You already knew that he was going to pull out just the right arrow for his moment of need. Never mind that the Boxing Glove Arrow was as big as your head and couldn't possibly fit in that quiver. Don't ponder the infinite number of arrows squeezed into that quiver. Never question how Green Arrow could always lay his hand on the right shaft in a split second. Forget all that. The fun lay in discovering what outlandishly unexpected arrow was coming next.

Unlikely as it may seem, God has a great deal in common with Green Arrow. As a matter of fact, the Old Testament writers often imagine God as a divine archer in the heavens aiming arrows at the earth. Sometimes God shoots arrows of vengeance and justice: "[God] will bend and string his bow. He has prepared his deadly weapons; he makes ready his flaming arrows" (Ps. 7:12–13). On other occasions God brings forth the arrow of salvation, as in this passage where the Messiah speaks: "In the shadow of his hand he hid me; he made me into a polished arrow and concealed me in his quiver" (Isa. 49:2).

This is not our usual way of thinking about God. Even though the idea comes straight from the Bible, I'll bet you've never heard a single sermon on God the Archer! But if God is truly the heavenly bowman, then it must follow that God has a bottomless quiver equipped with precisely the right arrows for every occasion. Enter Green Arrow!

Not only does God provide for us, but God apparently loves trick arrows. You never know what God is going to do next. Consider some of the off-the-wall ways in which God met Israel's needs in those wonderful Old Testament stories. For instance, there were the frogs and the boils and the burning hail. There was the brass snake on the pole, the trick walking stick that turned into a snake, and the other walking stick that blossomed with fresh flowers. God saved Israel from the Arameans with sound effects in the dark, and God took care of the Midianites with a destructive loaf of barley bread. Then there was the hornet attack, the soggy sheepskin, the ravens delivering groceries, the angry mother bear, the jar of oil that refused to run dry, and the sandals that never wore out. Oh, and let's not forget the talking donkey.

175

On the whole, these two things are consistently true in the Bible: (1) God provides for the faithful, and (2) God provides in unexpected ways, sometimes in ways that seem utterly inadequate at the moment.

For example, remember when Israel was stymied at the Red Sea with Pharaoh's army closing in? God loosed the Fan Arrow and a mighty wind blew all night long. The Israelites had to be scratching their heads and asking, "What do we need with wind? We can't even get our tents set up. This is the help you're sending us, God?" But next morning the Israelites discovered that the wind had driven back the sea and dried a path across the muddy seabed. To Israel's surprise, the Fan Arrow was exactly what they needed.

Consider the time Israel was going into battle against the Canaanites in the Esdraelon Valley. Everything was riding on this battle. The Israelites had barely managed to hang on to their foothold in the Promised Land. In fact, they were hiding in the hills because that was the only place they were safe from the Canaanite chariots. Chariots were the cutting edge of military technology. The Canaanites had them—iron chariots, in fact—and Israel didn't. When God told the Israelites to go face the Canaanites in the valley, the Jews were understandably skeptical. The valley was broad and flat, a perfect battlefield for chariots.

The battle began. The Israelites could not possibly survive the fight. The chariots were going to grind them into the ground. That's when God fired the Rain Arrow. The heavens started pouring. The Israelite soldiers were probably thinking, "Thanks so much, God. Not only must we fight a losing battle, but now we get to be wet and cold before we die!" But the rain softened the ground. The River Kishon overflowed its banks and flooded the plain. The valley floor turned into mud. When the battle began, no one could guess what God was up to, but you can guess what happened to those iron chariots in the soupy mud. Israel prevailed thanks to the Rain Arrow.

A few generations later the great threat was the Philistines, and again it was a matter of technology. The Philistines knew how to work iron; the Israelites didn't. The Israelite bronze weapons were utterly outclassed by Philistine iron. In an earlier chapter I mentioned Israel's need, but I didn't explain the unlikely circumstances through which God provided for that need.

At that time, Saul was the Jewish king. Saul was insane—and insanely jealous of Israel's best general, a young man named David. Saul drove David from his court and chased him into the wilderness hoping to kill him. David actually had to take refuge among the Philistines, pretending to become a traitor to his own people. David was a man to trust God, but surely he wondered why God wasn't giving him some help in those dark days.

He needn't have worried. David did eventually return to Israel. He became king, and suddenly the inventory of iron weapons in Israel grew like wildfire. Bible scholars believe that during his time among the Philistines, David spied out the secret of working iron, which he brought back with him. Who could have dreamed that a murderous, paranoid king and a bitter exile in the camp of the enemy would provide the Israelites with precisely the skill they needed to face the Philistine threat? Who would have imagined it? God, of course. God obviously thought it through and carried it through.

## The God with Perfect Aim

These biblical stories are interesting, but I can also tell stories closer to home. One of the beloved saints in our congregation died while I was away on vacation. I had been Elmer's pastor for nearly twenty-five years. Both his family and the congregation desperately wanted me there to lead the memorial service. Unfortunately, no one could reach me. I was camping with my family. Not even the church secretary knew exactly where we were, and we didn't have a phone with us. Regretfully, the family asked another pastor to preach the funeral.

Had our vacation unfolded as planned, we would have returned home the day after Elmer's funeral. Apparently, God had other plans. In our many years of camping, that was the wettest week we ever endured. We had torrential rain nearly every day. The sleeping bags were wet and the tents were molding. Campfires smoldered and sputtered. Towels never dried. I wanted to stick it out anyway, but the family outvoted me and we came home a day early, damp and dispirited. I had been deeply in need of rest and recreation, and I was terribly disappointed that our camping trip was such a bust.

We got home after midnight, and not until the next morning did I check our answering machine messages. At 8:00 a.m. I learned that the funeral was scheduled for 10:00 a.m.! I hurriedly scraped off a week of grime and whiskers, and I arrived at the church fifteen minutes before the service began. I can't recall another time when people were so happy to see me. When I walked through the door, the family took turns embracing me with laughter and tears.

I insisted the visiting pastor preside at the service as planned, but I joined in. I was able to speak from the heart about a man I had known and loved for decades and to tell firsthand stories about his faith and service. At the cemetery one woman took me aside and hugged me. Amid tears she said, "God sent that rain to wash you back here where you needed to be." A couple of days earlier, shivering in a wet sleeping bag, I had been miffed that God would rain on my camping trip, but in retrospect I am thankful for the Rain Arrow that brought me home in time.

God provides for us, and often in ways that leave us breathless with surprise. I realize hanging on to that certainty can be tough. Family turmoil, financial setbacks, medical problems—these things can rock our faith. How we weather those storms depends on what kind of God we trust.

When our back is to the Red Sea, the Punisher might well decide that we're about to receive exactly what we deserve. When the iron chariots are rumbling toward us, Galactus may figure we're not worth saving, and Odin could sleep through the whole battle. When we are lost, the Watcher may tell us that we'll have to handle this one on our own.

But Green Arrow won't let us down. He has strung his bow and fitted the shaft to the string. Even now he is taking aim. He always has the right arrow and he never misses the mark. That's a picture of God I can carry in my heart.

Who needs the Punisher when the Archer is watching over us?

# 13 Captain America
## Shielded from Sorrow

The paralysis grenade whizzes at my head, but I deflect it with a deft flick of my shield. A second grenade hurtles toward my chest at such incredible speed that I expect to hear a sonic boom. Instead my laughter booms as, in the face of certain death, I raise my shield again, ricocheting the deadly missile back at my attacker. Occasionally I dodge one of the missiles and it bounces off the brick wall at my back, but most of them I drive away with the shield. I love watching the grenade approach and then raising my shield at the last possible moment to send a bomb careening away harmlessly.

Invulnerability is so gratifying.

The dastardly Red Skull will have to do much better if he hopes to vanquish me, the fighting spirit of democracy!

Actually the grenades are only rubber balls thrown by my little brother Rod. The shield is a garbage can lid, the old-fashioned, galvanized metal kind, this one dented and smelly, but the grubbiness disappears as I grip the handle to wield the lid. I have been transformed from an eleven-year-old kid into the living legend of World War II. No matter what the enemy throws at me, I am fearless.

I am secure.

I am Captain America!

My mother comes into the backyard to hang the wet laundry. She shakes her head and mutters, "A whole house

180

full of toys, and he plays with a garbage can lid."

Of course she doesn't get it. She thinks this is just a game. Rod and I know better. Danger is serious business, and a good shield makes all the difference. True, I have other superhero devices: the Ka-Zar rope swing, the Creeper obstacle course, and the Superman two-step flying leap with a tablecloth cape tied around my neck. But grenade bouncing and the shield workout is one of my favorites—like an X-Men training session in the Danger Room.

## A Persistent Longing for Safety

Deflecting danger is a time-honored power among superheroes and villains alike. One of Captain America's patriotic cousins, the Shield, has a magnetic deflector sewn into his costume. First the deflector draws the bullets, and then it bounces them away. Brainiac 5 has a belt that generates an impenetrable force field. (Force fields are always impenetrable in the comics. What good is a penetrable force field?) Invisible Woman generates unseen barriers by sheer mental power. Unus the Untouchable is also Unus the imperturbable as knives, bullets, and bombs are repelled without touching his body.

But Captain America's shield was the best danger deflector of all. The disc featured concentric red and white stripes encircling a star in the center; it was created during World

181

War II by American scientists under top-secret conditions in an accidental process that no one has ever replicated. It is made of two remarkable components found only in the Marvel universe. The first part of the shield's unique alloy is adamantium, the hardest metal in existence, which is bonded to the second part—vibranium, a rare metal that absorbs shocks and vibrations. The more energy directed at vibranium, the tighter the bonds between the metal's molecules.

The upshot of this pseudoscience is the conviction that Captain America's shield is utterly indestructible. As long as he's holding the shield, Cap is indestructible, too. (Those of us on intimate terms with the good Captain often call him Cap.) Over the years, Cap's shield has protected him from grenades, explosions, lasers, boomerangs, spears, swords, arrows, sonic blasts, machine-gun fire, flame throwers, knives, and even the gamma-powered fist of the incredible Hulk.

Captain America is one of the grand old men of the superhero realm. Without belittling either his strength or his courage, the shield is essential to the character. Without the shield, Cap would be indistinguishable from a legion of red-white-and-blue patriotic heroes. The shield is his greatness.

Even the youngest comic reader knows that life is risky. Comics reassure us that courage and resourcefulness can overcome danger. Even if we don't want to admit it, adults long for the same assurance. That's why danger followed by struggle leading to victory is the basic storyline for so many popular books, movies, and television programs. (When was the last time you enjoyed a movie in which the hero got killed in the end?)

Captain America's shield represents a persistent human longing for safety and protection from the dangers and perils

182

of life in an uncertain world. That shield also reminds us of a claim that Christians make both glibly and routinely. The words may differ, but the substance is always the same:

"God will protect you."
"The Lord is your keeper."
"God takes care of his own."
"Don't be afraid. God is in charge."
"Christ will heal you."

Are Christians guaranteed a life without tragedy? Is an indestructible shield guarding us from cancer, birth defects, broken marriages, bankruptcy, car accidents, drive-by shootings, food poisoning, and tidal waves? If we are not shielded from these things, does that mean God's not taking care of us?

## What Good Is God As a Shield?

The Bible makes wonderful promises and bold, sweeping statements of encouragement about God's overarching protection of the faithful.

"The Lord is your keeper," the psalmist writes, "the Lord is your shade at your right hand. The sun shall not strike you by day, nor the moon by night. The Lord will keep you from all evil; he will keep your life" (Ps. 121:5–6 NRSV).

The apostle Paul was certainly a devoted and sincere follower of Jesus. He spent most of his adulthood preaching the gospel, founding churches, and encouraging other Christians. Paul wasn't perfect, but if anyone had a right to claim God's shielding power, Paul was the one. Yet Paul endured beatings, stonings, shipwrecks, privations, lynch mobs, betrayals, and a persistent physical ailment that he referred to as his "thorn in the flesh."

Ah, you say, but Paul came through every one of those ordeals. God was watching over him!

Yes, the apostle survived for many years, and the New Testament is silent as to Paul's fate, but ancient tradition assures us that Paul was executed for his faith—beheaded for proclaiming Christ in Rome.

Where was Paul's shield when the blade fell?

The New Testament does document other examples of early believers whose faith cost their lives: Stephen, the first martyr of the fledgling Christian movement, was stoned to death by an enraged mob. James the son of Zebedee was put to the sword by Herod Agrippa. James the brother of Jesus was stoned and clubbed to death. And if ancient traditions are reliable, of Jesus's twelve disciples, only John died of old age. The rest were stoned, burned, flayed, or stabbed for their loyalty to Christ.

And consider how Jesus himself died. After being betrayed and forsaken by his own disciples, Jesus was unjustly convicted on the basis of perjured testimony. On the way to Golgotha he was humiliated, whipped, and pierced with thorns. He hung in agony on a cross as the crowning blow fell: His enemies gathered round and laughed, their mockery raising a challenge to God's protective care.

"He trusts in God," the priests jeered. "Let God rescue him now" (Matt. 27:43).

In view of how Jesus suffered and died, surely we cannot claim that God always protects the faithful from pain and death. A skeptic might conclude that God's protection is like a cheap insurance policy that only covers us when we don't need it. But even if God doesn't exempt us from every calamity, this doesn't disprove the reality of God's shielding presence in life. Surely faith is not a suit of supernatural armor that guarantees our safety in all circumstances. Perhaps God has good reason for allowing occasional hardship and danger to afflict us.

How can we explain both the reality of risk and the reliability of God?

In the classical myths, heroes are usually tested severely before they reach their full stature. Even comic-book heroes follow this pattern. Peter Parker became the amazing Spider-Man after the murder of his beloved Uncle Ben. Daredevil gained his powers in an accident that robbed him of his sight. Iron Man was invented to overcome the accident that damaged Tony Stark's heart. Green Arrow learned his skill with the bow after being stranded on a deserted island. Wonder Woman and the Amazons of Paradise Island grew strong because of their earlier captivity to Hercules. Jim Corrigan was murdered on the eve of his wedding; only afterward could he take up the mantle of the Spectre.

We could just as easily make a long list of real people who have achieved heroic stature through overcoming childhood diseases, crippling accidents, poverty, and a host of other hardships.

When asked to name some of the best times in her life, an acquaintance of mine spoke of the dark days after the death of her son. Seeing the surprise on my face, she said, "You asked about the best times, not the most pleasant. That was a bitter and heartbreaking experience, but nothing else in my life has led to so much growth or taught me as much about God and myself."

Could it be that suffering serves a vital purpose, that God has good reason to allow some hardships into our lives? What if risk and struggle are necessary for our growth as human beings? Maybe hardship is the school that teaches us to become our best selves.

Some years ago I planted a runt ash tree in our side yard. One spring day when the tree was no more than six feet tall, a storm crashed through our neighborhood and literally bent the tree double like an upside-down *U*. The trunk was unbroken, but the crown of the tree lay on the soggy ground. During a lull in the storm, I straightened the tree and staked it against the wind.

Unfortunately, the wind shifted and the poor tree was once again bent double, this time in the opposite direction. To my surprise, not only did the tree survive this beating, but after the storm the runt grew like crazy. By fall the trunk had doubled in size. The struggle to survive energized that tree far more than my regular waterings or fertilizer feedings.

No one welcomes difficulties, but when we reflect upon our journey we find that the hard times made us stronger, wiser, and more compassionate. Without real risk there is no struggle, and without struggle why would we grow? Jellyfish float with the current and eat whatever comes within reach. Dolphins swim against the tide, hunt for their food, battle their enemies, and sometimes die in fishing nets. Dolphins have a much tougher life than jellyfish, but which would you rather be?

What about love? Imagine a world in which God miraculously rescues us from every danger. God catches the car as it goes off the bridge. God scoops us from the waves when the boat overturns. God zaps the cancer cells as soon as they are diagnosed. God halts the plane before it strikes the tower. In such a world how would we relate to God? We might love him, but wouldn't it be because he took care of us? How strong and tested would that love be? How would we know that his love—and ours—could stand up in spite of hardship and disappointment? We would never learn to love God for God's own sake.

In the prologue to the biblical book of Job, God and Satan have a conversation about upright Job. Satan sneers that Job only serves God because it is in his best interest to do so. God has prospered Job and shielded him from every setback. Satan implies that Job's love doesn't count for much because it comes so easily. To give the devil his due, Satan makes a good point. The rest of the book describes Job's struggle to hang on to God in spite of poverty, bereavement, and sickness. By the end of the book, Job has become a bigger person and his love has a dimension that was missing before.

Do you want to be loved only for the sake of what you can give to others? Nor does God want our love on that basis. The most perfect love has a no-matter-what, through-thick-and-thin quality. Real love will not write off God when things turn sour. Real love survives even when we are disappointed or angry with God. In a painless world, we would never learn the devoted love that prays, "Not my will but yours!"

That prayer contains one more crucial thing about suffering: At least sometimes, what appears to be a bad loss turns out to be a good thing.

I've discovered this lesson many times in life; in fact, one more time recently when our basement flooded. After the initial shock, we realized the damage was minimal. We salvaged the carpeting, and no furniture was lost; our televisions and computers remained dry too. Unfortunately, I had stored a couple of boxes of comic books in one corner of the basement, and they were ruined. Several thousand dollars worth of early *Spider-Man*, *Avengers*, *X-Men*, and *Fantastic Four* comics were reduced to soggy pulp.

I was devastated. As we vacuumed water out of the carpeting, I tallied the loss in my head. I reviewed the key books ruined by the flood. I kicked myself for stupidly storing comic boxes on the basement floor. What a terrible waste!

Or so I thought until I inventoried the boxes. Actually, none of my personal collection was stored in the basement. The waterlogged books were extras and duplicates left over from college days when I ran a small mail-order back-issue business to help pay tuition. Those boxes held stock I hadn't looked at in fifteen years. In that time the books had increased dramatically in value. I had always meant to sell them, but marketing to collectors required more time and patience than I had available, and selling to a dealer would have netted me half their value at best.

The flood solved my problem. The insurance company paid me full market value for the books. Then the agent sold the damaged books for a pittance to my local comic shop. The shop made a quick profit selling the damaged books, and local collectors got some great comics that normally would have been priced out of reach. Everybody was happy, and the insurance company still made money that year.

Admittedly, soggy comics are a trivial example of suffering. But most of us can cite weightier blows that turned into blessings. A broken wedding engagement opens the way for a healthier relationship with someone new. A lost job frees us to pursue the career of which we had only dreamed. A serious illness invites us to confront old grievances. Financial calamity strengthens the ties in a stale marriage. Such stories are too commonplace to be remarkable. The burden we despise today may become the very thing we celebrate tomorrow.

## The Invisible Edges

What if God shields us far more often than we realize? At the drop of a hat, many people can recite a catalogue of the bad things that have happened to them. But can we list the bad things that didn't happen to us?

Last summer my daughter and I visited Scotland and Wales. I have made several trips to Great Britain and am well aware of how the traffic flows there, but one afternoon in Edinburgh my mind must have been in neutral. I stepped off the curb into busy downtown traffic while looking in the wrong direction. In the best cartoon tradition I was nearly pancaked by a speeding double-decker bus. As I stuck one foot into the street, my daughter screamed, the bus horn blared, and I came as close to dying as I can ever recall. I teetered off balance while the bus blew past me, whipping my hair and nearly brushing my outstretched fingers. A difference of two inches or two seconds could have turned a summer holiday into a brutal tragedy.

Of course, I can't prove that God grabbed my sleeve that day, but I can't deny it either. Once my heartbeat returned to normal, I found myself wondering how many times God has yanked me out of the line of fire without my knowing it. The wobbly ladder that didn't fall, the infection that didn't take hold, the slip on the ice that left me bruised instead of paralyzed—such things are in the realm of "what if," and we mere mortals have no window into that domain. For all we know, God intervenes for our protection dozens of times every day.

The Spectre is one of the most powerful beings in the superhero world, an earth-bound spirit working for God on the mortal plane. Created by Jerry Siegel (one half of the creative team that dreamed up Superman), the Spectre had adventures ranging from cosmic to mundane. Sometimes the Spectre juggled whole planets. At other times he moved invisibly and silently behind the scenes in ordinary events. Some of the Spectre's most humorous stories involved the unseen spirit helping a comical, inept detective. The bumbling cop survived deadly attacks and solved crimes thanks to "lucky breaks" and "coincidences." He never knew that a powerful guardian tinkered with his daily life, shielding him from danger and guiding him toward success.

Neither can we always detect God's hand at work in our lives. One day while sitting at my kitchen table I noticed a praying mantis inside on the windowsill, apparently carried in with some garden vegetables. The attention of the mantis was fixed on an ant on the other side of the window glass. The ant crept innocently along the glass on the outside while the mantis stalked it on the inside. Again and again the mantis lunged for the ant, only to bounce off the glass. Eventually the ant disappeared from view and the forlorn mantis stared after it in perplexity.

I wonder how many times I have been that oblivious ant while God shielded me from danger I never suspected.

"I will not leave you as orphans; I will come to you," Jesus promised (John 14:18). Given that, maybe the essence of God's protection is the promise of God's presence. God may not always stand between us and the storm, but at the very least God will always stand beside us through the storm. The abiding presence of our Lord allows us to grow into our strength and gives us someone to lean on when our own strength is insufficient.

A friend told me about hitting bottom some years ago. His wife had left him because he was an addict. Late at night my friend went to bed in the empty house, but he couldn't sleep. Overcome by grief, loss, and self-hatred, he lay in the dark weeping. He squeezed his pillow and pressed it to his chest. Somehow he got the notion that his pillow was God's little finger. He wrapped himself around that pillow and held on for dear life. He decided that if God was with him, maybe he could make it through the night.

"I was lost in the dark," he said, "but I survived because I knew I wasn't alone in the dark."

"Surely I am with you always," Jesus promised (Matt. 28:20). If Jesus went to the cross for us, he is strong enough to walk beside us through any fire. He will hold our hand in the deepest waters. Life can lay us low, but there is no hell in which Christ would ever forsake us. It's like a scene in that humorous Image series called *Ball and Chain*, where a husband and wife gain superpowers but with one catch: Their powers only work when they are together. Our experience as Christians is similar. In trying times we discover that the nearness of Christ gives us far greater strength than we could muster alone.

## A New View of Protection

The X-Man Wolverine is one of the most popular characters Marvel has introduced in decades. Outwardly, Wolverine is unimpressive. He measures a mere five feet three inches. He doesn't fly or have super strength; he can't move at super speed or throw bolts of raw energy. Wolverine's powers are hidden within himself.

As a result of extensive surgery, Wolverine's skeleton is laced with adamantium. (Remember adamantium? It's the same stuff from which Captain America's shield was forged.) Thanks to this inward gift, Wolverine's skeleton is virtually unbreakable. He withstands attacks that would destroy a normal person.

Coupled with the adamantium skeleton, Wolverine has a second gift hidden within himself. He was born with a mutant ability for rapid healing. For instance, a bullet wound to a non-vital part of Wolverine's body will heal completely within an hour.

Wolverine is one tough customer. His adamantium skeleton makes him very hard to kill, and any wound that doesn't kill him will heal quickly. The scrappy mutant has been shot, sliced, gassed, poisoned, and impaled, but like his namesake he keeps coming. In one adventure Wolverine was riddled with bullets and severely burned over most of his body and then had the flesh blasted from one arm down to bare adamantium bones—all within twenty-four hours. At the end of the day he was still swinging.

This, after all, is Wolverine's chief heroic quality—the ability to keep on keeping on. He feels pain just as keenly as anyone else, but he knows he can survive the pain and come through to the other side.

When we think about God's protection, we need to remember both Wolverine and Captain America. Sometimes God's protection is an unbreakable shield deflecting the dangers that would destroy us. At other times God's protection is the sustaining inward strength that sees us through and heals us afterward.

Paul had this inner power in mind when he wrote, "Therefore we do not lose heart. Though outwardly we are wasting away, yet inwardly we are being renewed day by day" (2 Cor. 4:16). God always knows what we need, and God unfailingly provides for both our protection and growth.

Yet at least one last tough question demands an honest answer. Sometimes God neither deflects the bullet nor gives us the strength to survive it. What about the trials leading not to growth but to death? What shall we say when the cancer wins in spite of prayer, determination, and chemotherapy? What about the twenty-five-year-old mother killed by a brain aneurysm or the child who drowns at a birthday pool party? In the face of such naked tragedy, we dare not mouth easy assurances or pat answers.

Even so, we confess our hope in a God who is bigger than this world and whose power to heal is not limited to this world. We believe in a refuge where death has no more power, a bright place where no shadows fall. Without any proof whatsoever, we maintain that death does not get the last word.

In the world of comic books, death is a feeble foe. Both heroes and villains routinely return from the dead as if the great veil had been replaced with a revolving door. This year's heroic death is likely to become next year's "surprise" return from the grave. Comic book readers have become jaded on the subject. Longtime superhero fans don't take death seriously.

Perhaps we shouldn't give death too much weight in the real world either. We must respect grief and bereavement, but not death. Indeed, if we could see the "real world" as it truly is, we would discover that death is a defeated enemy. The grave has no final power over those who have given their lives to Christ.

As we saw earlier, the apostle Paul was acquainted first-hand with hardship. Yet Paul asserts, "I consider that our present sufferings are not worth comparing with the glory that will be revealed in us" (Rom. 8:18).

As surely as a trusty garbage can lid protected me from the rubber balls my little brother used to throw at me, God can and will protect his children from anything life throws our way.

We are not afraid! An adamantium shield goes before us, adamantium strength rises within us, and a golden city awaits us.

193

# 14 The Spirit
## The Gospel in a Nutshell

**W**hat a trip so far! We've visited Krypton, Paradise Island, and Asgard. We've survived gamma bombs, cosmic radiation, alien invasions, and even radioactive spider bites. We've strode and soared alongside scores of super-powered titans. But there are two more heroes yet to visit who deserve a larger following than any acquired so far. Let's start with Will Eisner's quirky crime fighter from the 1940s: the Spirit.

When the Spirit debuted for the American public on June 2, 1940, he had no powers and no costume except an overcoat and a domino mask. Actually, the Spirit didn't even have a real comic book. His weekly seven-page adventures were published as an insert in the Sunday newspaper. What the Spirit did offer readers was style, originality, humor, and the creative genius of writer and artist Eisner. Professionals and discerning fans have appreciated Eisner's work for decades; *The Spirit* series, reprinted in various formats over the years, is finally being collected in high-quality hardcover volumes.

Beyond the book's artistic merits, *The Spirit* is a personal favorite of mine for how its very first story unintentionally presents a condensed crash course in Christian theology. Consider the origin of the Spirit himself: Denny Colt is a young, brash criminologist out to make a name for himself by capturing the notorious international criminal Dr. Cobra.

Colt knows where Dr. Cobra is hiding and tips off his friend Dolan, the grizzled police commissioner. But Colt, determined to nab the evil scientist (and the reward money!) on his own, insists on a head start.

He follows Cobra's trail through shadowed alleys and underground passages; when he catches up with the mass murderer, Dr. Cobra is adding the final chemical ingredients to an enormous glass beaker filled with bubbling green liquid. As Colt fights to capture the villain, a gunshot shatters the glass globe, and the mysterious concoction drenches Colt, knocking him to the floor.

By the time Commissioner Dolan and the police arrive, Dr. Cobra has fled and Denny Colt lies immobile in a green chemical pool. A saddened Dolan calls the coroner, who pronounces Denny Colt dead. Within hours Colt is interred in the family tomb at Wildwood Cemetery, and Dolan resumes his efforts to capture Dr. Cobra.

Some nights later a mysterious figure enters the commissioner's office through an open window. The intruder hides his face in the shadows and informs Dolan that he intends to bring Cobra to justice before morning. The stranger declines to give his name, identifying himself only as the Spirit. Dolan thinks he recognizes the voice of the mystery man and tails him when he leaves.

Of course, the Spirit turns out to be Denny Colt, back from the dead. The strange formula of Dr. Cobra had induced a death-like state, and Denny Colt later awoke in the family crypt. For the time being he decides to keep his identity a secret so that Dr. Cobra will not be forewarned of his return.

This time Colt makes good on his promise to apprehend Dr. Cobra. When the crime fighter turns Dr. Cobra over to Dolan, the commissioner asks Colt what he plans to do next. Will he take his sensational story to the papers?

No, the Spirit confides. He's now free of the law's constraints since in the eyes of the law Denny Colt is dead. The masked man will let his former identity lie—he'll leave Denny Colt dead and begin a new life as the Spirit. He'll devote himself to catching the criminals who escape through legal loopholes. Freed from the letter of the law, the Spirit can now fulfill the intention of the law.

## The Ultimate Escape

If the apostle Paul had written comic books instead of letters, he might have penned the origin of the Spirit. The Spirit's origin story is like the gospel in a nutshell, and it allows one to think of Denny Colt as a kind of every-disciple, a stand-in for all Christians. Colt is plunged beneath the waters of baptism and dies to his former life. His old self passes away, dead and buried, so that he might become an entirely new person.

In Paul's words, "For we died and were buried with Christ by baptism. And just as Christ was raised from the dead by the glorious power of the Father, now we also may live new lives" (Rom. 6:4 NLT).

Furthermore, in his new identity the Spirit is liberated from the power of the law. Dying to the law carries very practical benefits. If Denny Colt had any outstanding parking tickets or library overdue fines, his death cancels those obligations. From the day the Spirit walks out of his tomb in Wildwood Cemetery, he has a new life of freedom and fresh possibilities.

Since Paul didn't write comic books, he decided to say it this way: "The law no longer holds you in its power, because you died to its power when you died with Christ on the cross" (Rom. 7:4 NLT). Paul doesn't say this because he's got some beef with the law; if law and order were no good, a lot of superheroes would be wasting their time.

No, in fact, Paul loves God's law. But Paul knows that no one is able to fulfill the law perfectly. Following the rules will get us into heaven only if we keep every rule every time—and nobody does. Nobody can. Our sins and mistakes have run up a massive debt to the law, a debt we have no means to pay. God offers us a way out, a way that we can die in the eyes of the law and become as new and debt-free as Eisner's Spirit.

## The Ultimate Freedom

Look again at the story of Denny Colt, this time as a retelling of the story of Jesus Christ. Like Denny Colt tracking down the murderous Cobra, the Savior comes to end the reign of terror of "that ancient serpent, who is the Devil" (Rev. 20:2 NRSV). No one else has been able to overcome this serpentine figure of evil.

Indeed, so powerful is the devil that even Jesus is seemingly defeated. God's Son dies on a cross, apparently one more helpless victim of the powers of darkness.

Once Jesus is laid in the tomb, his loved ones mourn him and his enemies dismiss him. Friends and foes alike assume the story is finished. To the amazement of everyone, Jesus emerges from the tomb three days after his death. Christ has turned defeat into victory. The one who was dead is alive again and lives forevermore. Christ's resurrection overthrows his ancient enemy and vanquishes the power of sin and death.

Christ is willing and able to share this victory with others. Anyone who fully trusts him, instead of relying upon the law, becomes a shareholder. Baptism is the visible sign of our commitment to Christ as well as Christ's commit-

197

ment to us. Symbolically our old, sinful selves share the death of Jesus on the cross. In turn we also share the resurrection of Jesus, becoming new people and receiving a new nature. "And just as Christ was raised from the dead by the glorious power of the Father, now we also may live new lives" (Rom. 6:4 NLT).

New Testament writers offer several ways to picture what Jesus did on the cross: as a price paid to ransom us from captivity to death, as the sacrificial lamb whose blood washes away our sins, and as an innocent who's stood up in the courtroom to take upon himself the guilty sentence pronounced upon you and me.

Each of these ideas illuminates the meaning of Jesus's death and resurrection, but my favorite is the so-called "battle image" of the crucifixion—the cross as the scene of the ultimate showdown between good and evil. I'm not alone in choosing this metaphor. "In this way," Paul writes, "God disarmed the evil rulers and authorities. He shamed them publicly by his victory over them on the cross of Christ" (Col. 2:15 NLT).

Who isn't a sucker for this kind of no-holds-barred, good-versus-evil slugfest? Quick—name fifty great comic book battles while standing on your head . . .

Thor versus the invincible Destroyer. Yes.

Orion's epic struggle with his father Darkseid. Uh huh.

Captain America battling the Red Skull and the cosmic cube. Right.

The duel between Dr. Strange and Dracula. Good.

The Justice League of America tangling with the Crime Syndicate. Keep going.

Iron Man clashing with Dr. Doom.

The Spectre making war on Azmodus, hurling whole planets as missiles . . .

198

What makes these battles classic is the clear delineation of righteousness and wickedness, the no-quarter stakes, the courage of the outmatched champion, and the unlikelihood of the hero's victory. Like half the great stories of humankind, these war tales depict the epic struggle between good and evil.

Yet the war fought on the cross overshadows all the battles of myth, legend, and history. The difference: Saving the world is commonplace in comic books, but the battle outside the walls of Jerusalem nearly two thousand years ago was real. Few realized it at the time. None of the onlookers that day could see behind the scenes to the battle raging between heaven and hell. The human eye saw a thorn-crowned man dying in agony, nothing more. No one knew the fate of the world was up for grabs. Eternity hung in the balance. One broken, glorious hero stood his ground while the legions of hell did their worst. No victory was ever bought more dearly.

The outcome was never really in doubt, though. Satan is no match for God—not then, not now. Some Christians in the Middle Ages wondered where Jesus went between Good Friday and Easter. They created colorful stories of Christ storming the kingdom of hell, crashing through the great bronze gates, cowing the demons, and announcing his everlasting victory. Those fanciful stories remind us that no power in the universe can challenge God. This is why the Bible often speaks of God destroying evil with "the breath of his mouth" (Isa. 11:4; 2 Thess. 2:8).

That's how much effort God expends to overthrow the cosmic powers of evil. Just one breath and the kingdom of darkness is undone. In the contest between good and evil, there is no contest. Why then did Jesus go to the cross?

## The Ultimate Cost

If half the world's stories are about good overcoming evil, the other half are love stories. Both themes meet in the crucifixion. God purposely chose a means of salvation that would reveal the depths of God's love for us. The cross is his way of saying, "Look how much I love you! See how much you matter to me! You may break my heart, but you will never change my mind. No price is too high to pay for you, not even the death of my own Son."

Neither Roman soldiers nor all the armies of hell could hang Christ on the cross against his will. Nails didn't hold Jesus on the cross; love did. He is simply and plainly the superhero above all others. Christ paid the ultimate price, he won the decisive victory, and he did it all for love.

That love invites us to join his victory and unite with his cause. Following Jesus doesn't exempt us from pain and disappointment. Being his disciple is an adventure, and any true adventure involves risk and struggle. Sometimes the road is hard, but along the way Christ gives us the strength to meet whatever comes.

Writing to believers facing difficult trials, Paul admits that the way of faith is not necessarily the easiest path through life. He acknowledges a catalogue of troubles that Christians sometimes face: hardship, hunger, persecution, danger, even the sword. Paul asks if such tribulations have the power to separate us from Christ. Then he answers his own question in words that still ring across the centuries: "No, in all these things we are more than conquerors through him who loved us" (Rom. 8:37 NRSV).

Our English Bibles don't do justice to this passage. Writing in Greek, Paul knew he needed a powerful word to make his point. When he couldn't find the right word, he coined a new one—yes, made one up! He took the Greek word for "conquer" and he stuck onto the front of it the word "super." What Paul really says is that we "super-conquer" through Jesus Christ.

We are super-conquerors!

Troubles may batter us, but Jesus has already won our victory. He's assembling a team of heroes, and he invites us to join. For those who follow him, Jesus promises something better than safety. He promises adventure, abundant life, and certain victory. Best of all, Christ shares his power with his followers. Everyone who joins the team of this superhero becomes a super-conqueror.

Sometimes real life is better than comic books.

# What Superpowers Lurk inside You?

No two superheroes are exactly the same, and each one possesses different powers, weaknesses, and reactions. For instance, Spider-Man loves to wisecrack, but Batman never jokes. Wolverine is a loner at heart, while Captain America loves being a team player.

Who do you identify with most? What's your style? What are your strengths? What character traits would you call your Kryptonite—the tendencies you have (and we all have 'em) that debilitate you or hold you back from doing and being your best?

Once you identify these personality traits, you'll better understand why you do the things you do—and how your personality can empower and fuel your spiritual life.

Never fear, though. You don't need X-ray vision to find answers to these things.

This quiz is designed to help you see yourself just as you are. Take ten minutes to read through the following and reflect upon why you are the way you are and do the things you do.

Read the descriptions of each of the four pairs of superhero characters below. Which hero in each pair do you identify with most? Put a check mark next to that hero's name, then read the key on pp. 206–9 to learn more about your hidden (or not-so-hidden) superpowers and Kryptonite.

## DAZZLER VERSUS INVISIBLE WOMAN

☐ Dazzler is a mutant who turns sound energy into light. She loves to perform in front of a crowd, and the shouts of the audience feed her energy.

☐ Invisible Woman is the quiet member of the Fantastic Four. She doesn't draw attention to herself and though present may be missed or overlooked.

## DAREDEVIL VERSUS PROFESSOR X

☐ Daredevil's super senses and personal radar keep him in touch with everything going on around him. He finds meaning in the objective world of sound, smell, and texture.

☐ Professor X's telepathic powers allow him to read thoughts and mentally visit other planes of existence. He finds life and reality within his own inner world of ideas and thoughts.

## BATMAN VERSUS WONDER WOMAN

☐ Batman is a thinker and a planner. He analyzes a problem and solves it by applying rules and principles. He relies on logic. Emotions are merely a distraction.

❏ Wonder Woman trusts her feelings. She values love and peace, feeling that most problems are best solved with compassion and kindness.

## GREEN LANTERN VERSUS PLASTIC MAN

❏ Green Lantern's power ring allows this hero to re-shape reality according to his own ideas and needs. Green Lantern can change the world around him by the force of his will.

❏ Plastic Man constantly reshapes himself, taking any form that is handy and convenient at the moment. He is the JLA's resident clown, constantly changing shape to get a laugh.

## Key to Superhero Self-Quiz
# Revealing Your Secret Superpowers

You can't be right or wrong when it comes to personality. Just like superhero traits, personalities simply . . . are. But getting a handle on your own personality will help you in many ways. Knowing your strengths will help you discover the things that come easy for you and are the most satisfying. Figuring out your Kryptonite might help you avoid situations that lead to stress or failure. Also, the better you understand your own style in life, the more likely you can figure out why other people act the way they do.

Knowledge is a power! The better you know yourself, the more power you can tap for doing and becoming your best. As you look at the pairs of heroes below, try to think of specific insights that will help you get more out of life.

## DAZZLER VERSUS INVISIBLE WOMAN

If you're a Dazzler type, your superpower is teamwork and group building. You're sociable and outgoing, and you love interaction and group worship. But your Kryptonite is that you may sometimes lack inner depth and avoid being alone with God.

If you're an Invisible Woman type, your superpower is inner strength and reflection. You have strong personal values, are faithful in private prayer, and aren't afraid to stand apart from the crowd. Your Kryptonite, however, is sometimes you can be withdrawn and alienated from others, and you may resent intrusions and avoid taking action.

## DAREDEVIL VERSUS PROFESSOR X

If you're a Daredevil type, your superpower is an incredible awareness of the physical world. You are practical, have a desire to serve, are good with details, and appreciate God's good creation. But your Kryptonite is you don't cope well with confusion and uncertainty, and sometimes you act without having a good grasp of the big picture.

If you're a Professor X type, your superpower is imagination and intuition. You have fresh ideas and see how to change things, are hopeful, and often have a vision for a better future. Your Kryptonite, though, is sometimes you have so many ideas you never get around to putting them into practice. You may be so deep in your own inner world that you forget to offer service in the outer world.

## BATMAN VERSUS WONDER WOMAN

If you're a Batman type, your superpower is reason and logic. You have rules for life and follow them faithfully, and you can often find a solution just by thinking things

207

through. Your Kryptonite is that you can seem unfeeling or uncaring to others. You don't like bending the rules, even for a good cause, and sometimes you get tunnel vision.

If you're a Wonder Woman type, your superpower is emotional maturity and flexibility. You're in touch with feelings—both your own and others'—and you forge strong relationships. You know when to make an exception to the letter of the law in order to fulfill the spirit of the law. Your Kryptonite, however, is that sometimes you don't think things through, you rely too much on your gut instincts, and you may be unable to cope with conflict and confrontation.

## GREEN LANTERN VERSUS PLASTIC MAN

If you're a Green Lantern type, your superpower is initiative and hard work. You cause things to happen, are productive and systematic, and are driven to make a genuine difference in the world. Your Kryptonite is that you dislike disorder and chaos and sometimes can be a control freak.

If you're a Plastic Man type, your superpower is spontaneity and playfulness. Instead of changing the world, you respond to what's going on around you and adapt yourself to circumstances. Your Kryptonite is that you don't do well with deadlines, and systems or details bore you to death.

# Holy Heroes! What's It All Mean?

Take a look at how the superheroes you've just considered in the self-quiz might behave if they found themselves in an uncomfortably chilly room:

> Dazzler types will help everyone warm up by leading an exercise session.

208

Invisible Woman types will slip away quietly in search of a warmer room.

Daredevil types will be the first to notice that the room is cold and will know exactly where the draft is coming from.

Professor X types will mentally retreat to the warmth of an imaginary tropical island.

Batman types will calculate how much extra insulation the walls need and how best to install it.

Wonder Woman types will find someone who's cold and give that person a hug.

Green Lantern types will close the window or raise the thermostat.

Plastic Man types will put on a sweater—inside out, just for fun!

So, if you're a Dazzler-Daredevil-Wonder Woman-Plastic Man type: You might lead an ice breaker as you try to block the draft in the room and hug a helper while telling a joke about the jacket you're trying to put on with the arms tucked inside!

In any case, knowing your strengths and weaknesses can only help you in life, as you ask God to use them all for his good.

# Super Questions

# A Study Guide
# for Individual or Group Use

## Chapter 1—Superman: The Saving Son from Above

1. On our planet Superman is solar powered, drawing his powers from the sun in the heavens. From what source does Jesus draw his powers? Read Luke 4:14, 18–19; Matthew 12:28; and Acts 10:37–38.
2. What are some of the powers Jesus possesses? Read:

   - Matthew 8:23–27
   - Matthew 8:5–17; 9:1–8; and 9:18–35
   - Matthew 8:18–19 and 23–26, also John 11:1–44
   - Matthew 8:28–33 and Mark 3:7–11
   - Luke 5:17–26
   - Luke 24:36–40 and John 8:59
   - Mark 8:1–13; Luke 9:10–17; and John 2:1–11
   - Mark 15:32–16:18; Luke 24:1–40; and John 20

3. How does Jesus use his power for good? Re-read the passages above, noting the effects of each exercise of power. Also read Mark 10:45; Luke 9:52–56; and John 3:16–17.
4. How did Jesus wrestle with power? Read Matthew 4:1–11; Matthew 26:36–56; Luke 4:1–13; and Luke 22:39–46.

5. Is Jesus's choice about how to use his power superhuman? Read John 6:38; 9:4; and 10:15–18; Philippians 2:5–8; Hebrews 2:9–18; and Hebrews 10:12.
6. How is Jesus both human and superhuman/divine? Read Philippians 2:5–11; Colossians 2:8–10; Hebrews 1:1–4; and 1 John 4:9–10.
7. What does Jesus ultimately do with his power? Read Philippians 2:8.
8. What might we see if Jesus unleashed his power? Read Matthew 26:53; 28:18; and Revelation 1:7.

## Chapter 2—The Hulk: The Monster Within

1. Who is the Hulk—Bruce Banner's alter ego, his opposite, or another aspect of the real Bruce Banner?
2. Describe the Hulk. What makes him tick?
3. Can the Hulk be tamed, and if so, how? Subdued? Defeated?
4. Could you live with the Hulk? Alongside him?
5. Why is it so difficult to fight the Hulk and to struggle against sin? Read Ephesians 6:12.
6. What does the Hulk, like sin, demand? Read John 8:34.
7. The Hulk grabs everything for himself and always wants his own way. How is that like sin? Read Proverbs 16:5, 18; 8:13; 21:4; and 26:12. Where does following this path of sin or urge of the Hulk lead? Read Luke 9:24–25 and Proverbs 16:25.
8. Are we hopeless against the Hulk? Why or why not? Read Luke 11:18–22 and Colossians 2:13–15.
9. Who is the one superhero to conquer the Hulk and every other evil power? Read Ephesians 1:20–22 and 1 Corinthians 15:24–26.

## Chapter 3—Batman: Guilt and Grace in Gotham City

1. What drives Batman to avenge injustice?
2. What are Batman's greatest gifts and talents?
3. How is our human nature like Batman's nature? Read Proverbs 28:25, 30:12; and 1 Corinthians 10:12.
4. What would Jesus say to Batman if they were to meet in the night? Read Matthew 19:16–26 and John 3:1–21.
5. What does Jesus say to you about the worth found in service, good deeds, and setting right injustices? Read Colossians 3:17 and Romans 3:23, 27–28.
6. Do you seek the superpowers Jesus offers out of fear or true, genuine love? Explore Matthew 18:22–35. Are you like the wicked slave? Do you obey because you fear the consequences? Now read Luke 7:41–47. When are you like the woman who washes Jesus's feet with her tears?

211

7. What is one of the greatest superpowers found in grace? Read Ephesians 1:7; 2 Thessalonians 2:16; and 2 Timothy 1:8–10.
8. How is submission a superpower, and where is there strength in admitting one's need? Read Matthew 23:11–12 and James 4:10 and 5:16.
9. Where is the power and what is the good in accepting forgiveness? Read Luke 14:11; Ephesians 4:7–8; 1 Peter 2:18–25; 5:5–6, 10.

## Chapter 4—Iron Man: Salvation by Success

1. Why did Tony Stark devote his living to the invention of weapons for destruction?
2. What did he discover mattered more than creating the next big thing?
3. How was he humbled?
4. With what did Stark, aka Iron Man, try to arm himself for the ongoing battles in his life?
5. What are your ongoing battles? What armor do you find yourself reaching for most often?
6. What armor does an Old Testament soldier-king and a New Testament warrior-zealot say will never fail us? Read Psalm 28:7 and Ephesians 6:10–18.
7. Where can we find the healthy heart that Tony Stark, beneath all his inventions and protective metal, yearns for? Read Psalm 51:10 and Ezekiel 36:26.
8. Tony Stark had the friendship-unto-death of the old scientist Yinsen. Who in your life will step in when people, power, or even the greatest armor fails you? Read Hebrews 4:14–16 and 9:11–28.

## Chapter 5—Superman Revisited: Death, Resurrection, and Doomsday

1. Name some things Superman can do with his superpowers.
2. If you could have one of Superman's powers, which would you choose and how would you use it?
3. If you had all of Superman's powers, do you think you could save the world from war, selfishness, and hatred?
4. What's the one thing even the greatest superpower cannot eventually stop? Read Psalm 89:48 and Ecclesiastes 3:20.
5. Read the dictionary definitions of *rescue* and *save*. What is the difference between being rescued and being saved?
6. Read Jeremiah 38:7–13 and Acts 9:23–25. Are these stories about rescuing or saving? What about John 5:25–29?

7. Can you name some of the heroes in our world who rescue people in times of need? Have you ever been rescued? Have you ever been a rescuer?
8. Who alone has the power to truly save us from death? Read Acts 4:10–12 and 2 Timothy 1:10.

## Chapter 6—Wonder Woman: The Power of Truth

1. What are Wonder Woman's superpowers?
2. How is truth a weapon? Read John 8:32 and Ephesians 6:14.
3. List three or four practical situations in life when truth can be a powerful weapon.
4. How do lies enslave? Read Proverbs 12:13, 22; and 13:5–6.
5. Which is worse: the lies we tell to others or the lies we tell ourselves? Knowing both kinds of lies bear consequences, reflect upon Psalm 51:6; Ecclesiastes 5:2, 6; Zechariah 8:16; 1 John 1:5–10; James 5: 19–20; and Acts 5:1–11.
6. Are we truth-filled or lie-based creatures? Read Matthew 15:19; John 3:19; and 1 John 1:8.
7. Where can we find truth? Read John 1:14; John 14:6; and John 16:13.
8. Is there a difference between knowing the truth and living the truth? Read 2 John 4 and 3 John 3–4. What does the Bible mean by "walking in the truth"?
9. How can we live truth-fully? Read John 18:37 and John 8:31–32, 43–51.

## Chapter 7—Thor: Transformation

1. What is the nature of transformation? How does it work in the comic world?
2. How long does transformation last for superheroes in the comic world?
3. What about for us in real life? Read Ephesians 4:24.
4. Is transformation for the Christian something that just—Shazam!— happens? How much is up to us? Read Ephesians 4:13–15, 24.
5. How exactly does transformation happen for the Christian? Read Romans 12:2; 2 Corinthians 5:17–19; and Philippians 2:12–13.
6. How certain is transformation for the Christian? Read Romans 8:29 and 2 Peter 1:4.
7. When will the Christian be completely, forever transformed? Read 1 Corinthians 15:50–57.
8. What does transformation look like? Read 1 John 3:2.

## Chapter 8—Spider-Man: Saved for Service

1. What powers does Peter Parker gain as Spider-Man?
2. What does Spider-Man do with his powers?
3. Does God grant each of us special powers? Read 1 Corinthians 7:7 and 12:4–11.
4. Why are we given these gifts or powers? Read James 2:14 and 1 Peter 4:10.
5. What powers or gifts and talents do you feel you've been given? How are you exercising those powers?
6. Peter, the fisherman who became a great disciple of Christ, must have been surprised to find he had the gift of preaching. Do you think you might have powers you haven't discovered yet? Read and reflect upon Philippians 2:13.
7. In what ways can God use your powers or gifts even when you believe they've failed him? Read 2 Corinthians 8:12.
8. What is the reward of using your gifts—giving away yourself? Read Ecclesiastes 5:19–20.

## Chapter 9—Daredevil: Discernment

1. What are Daredevil's greatest gifts?
2. How are Daredevil's gifts like the Christian gift of discernment—the ability to tell the difference between the worthy and the worthless, the good and the bad?
3. Read the story of how Saul lost his sight and found his mission in Acts 9:1–19. How is Saul's story like Daredevil's? How is it different?
4. In Luke 18:35–42 you can read about a blind man who, like Daredevil, "saw" something others missed. If our senses will not lead us to Jesus, what will?
5. Daredevil's super hearing uncovers hidden truth. Jesus often ended his sermons with the words in Matthew 11:15. What do you think Jesus had in mind?
6. Daredevil has learned to "tune out" much of what goes on around him. For another example of tuning out, read Acts 28:26–27. How do people tune out God? Why would anyone do that?
7. How does the Bible teach us to practice discernment? Read Hebrews 5:14; 1 John 4:1; and 1 Thessalonians 5:21.

## Chapter 10—X-Men: In the World but Not of It

1. Consider the X-Men's great struggle—their search for belonging. Read 1 Peter 2:9–10. Where do Christians belong if not to the world?

214

2. Knowing his disciples would be at odds with the world, how did Jesus pray for his followers? Read John 17:14–19. What does truth have to do with being in the world but not belonging to the world?
3. What do you think is the best hope for different groups of people to be united? What does Ephesians 2:14–16 say about this?
4. When you reflect on the life of Jesus, do you think he "fit in" the world of his day? Do you think he fits in today's world?
5. In Matthew 11:18–19 Jesus talks about two distinct ways of being in the world. Can you describe those different ways?
6. Read Galatians 6:14. What do you think Paul means when he speaks of the world being crucified to him and he to the world?
7. Some of the ways Christians relate to the world are:

   • peaceful coexistence
   • withdrawing from worldly activities
   • overcoming the world
   • carrying the message of Jesus into the world

   Read James 1:27; 4:4; John 20:21; 1 John 5:4–5; and Romans 12:18 and match each passage with one way Christians deal with the world.

# Chapter II—The Fantastic Four: The Ties That Bind

1. Describe the Fantastic Four—who are they?
2. Identify qualities of the Fantastic Four that are like qualities of the church. Read Romans 14:19; Galatians 6:10; and Ephesians 2:19–22.
3. How did the Fantastic Four nurture and love one another into maturity?
4. How do members of the church nurture one another? Read Acts 2:44–46 and Hebrews 10:24–25.
5. Read Ephesians 4:25–32. Does this sound like a description of the Fantastic Four? Of the church? Why or why not?
6. If the church is a family, what is the basis of its family ties? Read Mark 3:31–35.
7. As the Fantastic Four find mutual strength living and working together, how can the church find its strength in community? Read Galatians 6:2; 1 Thessalonians 5:11–15; and 1 Peter 4:8–10.

# Chapter 12—The Punisher versus Green Arrow: What Is God Like?

1. What powers does the Punisher possess? What is his mission in life?
2. What is Galactus's strength? What is the driving force in his existence?

215

3. After reading 1 John 4:7–10, how would you express God's mission in the universe?
4. How is the Watcher powerful?
5. How can you know the true God sees more than the Watcher—beyond events and into your heart? Read Luke 12:6–7 and Psalm 56:8–11.
6. Would you say God is just an observer, or is God also a doer? Read Exodus 3:7–10; Deuteronomy 7:18–21; and Isaiah 46:3–4.
7. What does Odin, the All-Father of Asgard, seem to do with his power?
8. How is the God of the Bible different from Odin? Read Psalm 121:3 and Psalm 94:8–10.
9. Describe Green Arrow's powers.
10. How are the Punisher and the Green Arrow different in their quest for justice?

## Chapter 13—Captain America: Shielded from Sorrow

1. What good is a shield? Read Psalm 91. How many different ways does the psalmist describe God's protective power?
2. When have you longed for a shield?
3. A shield is old-fashioned protection. If you were going to talk about God's protective power in updated words, what terms might you use? (Hint: think about modern things like cars, computers, and skateboards.)
4. How is God like Captain America's shield? Read Psalm 121:5–6 and Psalm 46:1–3.
5. Is there proof that faithfulness and righteousness will not always shield us from misfortune? Read about John the Baptist (Mark 6: 17–29), Stephen (Acts 7:54–60), James (Acts 12:1–2), and Jesus (Mark 14:32–42).
6. What does that mean in light of promises such as those in Psalm 91?
7. What does it mean to call on, and receive, God's protection? Read Matthew 28:20 and John 14:18.
8. What if God's shielding were something to protect us from not only forces without but also gales within? Read 2 Corinthians 4:16. How does this broaden your view of what "God's protection" means?
9. Why does God want us to hold him as a shield anyway? Read Romans 8:18.

## Chapter 14—The Spirit: The Gospel in a Nutshell

1. Describe the liberation felt by Will Eisner's superhero Denny Colt once he realizes he's been transformed into the Spirit.

216

2. How is the Spirit's origin like a Christian's? Read Romans 6:3–11; Romans 7:4–6; and 1 Peter 3:21.
3. Are there things in your life to which you wish you were "dead"? Are there other things to which you wish you were more fully alive?
4. How was the cross a battleground? Read Colossians 1:19–20 and 2:15.
5. Like the Spirit, many superheroes gain their powers through events that seem terrible at the time. In the real world, can God use painful experiences to empower us and bring us into Jesus's "team"? Read Romans 8:28–29.
6. Read Matthew 10:39. How does the story of Denny Colt help us understand the meaning of Jesus's words in this passage?
7. Read John 5:24; 7:37–38; 10:10; 11:25–26; 2 Corinthians 5:17; and 1 John 5:1. Are these passages talking about different kinds of life or are these different ways of talking about the same gift of life?

217

# Acknowledgments

I owe thanks to many people for many reasons:

to Jan for faith and for the Alpha-Smart;

to Bethany and Rachel for enlarging my heart and interrupting my writing;

to Harvey and Gail Brewer for trips to the drugstore and quarters at the barbershop;

to Mark Johnson for chords and smoke rings in the last homely house;

to Cec Murphey for friendship and mentoring as well as patience when I fell behind on his plan;

to Kirk Burdick for years of artwork, and finally some for which I could pay him;

to Wayne Holmes for friendship, lunches, and many miles on the road;

to Sara Merrill for instilling in me a passionate love for words;

to countless comic book writers and artists for stretching my imagination;

to Paul, Cathy, and the gang at Comic Book World for running the world's finest comic shop;

to Kathy and Alan for the computer;

to the beloved saints at CSPC for letting me try out some of these chapters in the pulpit (and especially to Ian Boyd for interest and encouragement);

and for diverse reasons to Howard Shore, Tan Dun, Duffy Vohland, and the staff at the Erlanger Library.

# Notes

As yet there is no universally recognized format for annotating comic books. The matter is further complicated by the variety of formats in which comic stories are currently published. The style adopted here provides sufficient information for anyone who wishes to seek out the stories cited.

### Chapter 1 Superman

1. Michael Barrier and Martin Williams, eds., *A Smithsonian Book of Comic-Book Heroes* (New York: Smithsonian Institution Press and Harry N. Abrams, 1981), 19.

2. John Byrne, *Superman* #2, volume 2 (New York: DC Comics, February 1987), 22.

3. Paul Dini, *Wonder Woman: Spirit of Truth* (New York: DC Comics, 2001), unpaged.

### Chapter 2 The Hulk

1. Stan Lee, *The Incredible Hulk* #1 (New York: Marvel Comics, May 1962), 14.

2. Stan Lee, *The Incredible Hulk* #2 (New York: Marvel Comics, July 1962), 1.

3. Stan Lee, *The Incredible Hulk* #3 (New York: Marvel Comics, September 1962), 13.

4. Ibid., 14.

5. Stan Lee, *The Incredible Hulk* #5 (New York: Marvel Comics, January 1963), 24.

6. Stan Lee, *The Incredible Hulk* #2, 4.

7. From Walt Kelly's daily Pogo newspaper strip for Earth Day, March 21, 1971.

## Chapter 3  Batman

1. Roberta E. Pearson and William Uricchio, "Notes from the Batcave: An Interview with Dennis O'Neil," in *The Many Lives of the Batman*, ed. Roberta E. Pearson and William Uricchio (New York: Routledge, Chapman and Hall, 1991), 19.

2. Jim Starlin, *Batman* #428 (New York: DC Comics, December 1988), 2.

3. Jim Starlin, *Batman* #429 (New York: DC Comics, January 1989), 18.

4. Frank Miller, *Batman: The Dark Knight Returns – Book Four* (New York: DC Comics, 1986), 40.

5. Frank Miller, *Batman: The Dark Knight Returns – Book One* (New York: DC Comics, 1986), 18.

6. Frank Miller, *Batman: The Dark Knight Returns – Book Three* (New York: DC Comics, 1986), 26.

7. Frank Miller, *Batman: The Dark Knight Returns – Book One*, 42.

8. Ibid., 47.

## Chapter 4  Iron Man

1. Joe Quesada, *Iron Man: Mask in the Iron Man* (New York: Marvel Comics, 2001), unpaged.

2. Ibid.

## Chapter 5  Superman Revisited

1. Dan Jurgens, *Superman* #75 (New York: DC Comics, January 1993), unpaged.

2. Roger Stern, *The Death and Life of Superman* (New York: Bantam Books, 1993), 125.

## Chapter 6  Wonder Woman

1. Christopher Moeller, *JLA: A League of One* (New York: DC Comics, 2000), 13.

2. Les Daniels, *Wonder Woman: The Life and Times of the Amazon Princess* (San Francisco: Chronicle Books, 2000), 75.

## Chapter 7  Thor

1. Will Pfeifer, *H-E-R-O* #2 (New York: DC Comics, May 2003), 4.

2. Frank Miller, *The Dark Knight Strikes Again* #3 (New York: DC Comics, 2002), 5.

3. Cec Murphey's prayer is adapted from Macrina Wiederkehr, "A Prayer to Own Your Own Beauty," in *Seasons of the Heart* (San Francisco: Harper-SanFrancisco, 1991), 71.

## Chapter 8 Spider-Man

1. Stan Lee, *Amazing Fantasy* #15 (Marvel Comics, August 1962), 8.
2. Ibid., 11.
3. Stan Lee, *Fantastic Four* #1 (Marvel Comics, November 1961), 13.
4. Ibid.
5. Paul Dini, *Superman: Peace on Earth* (New York: DC Comics, 1999), unpaged.
6. Older comics included several brief stories in each issue.
7. Stan Lee, *Amazing Spider-Man* #33 (Marvel Comics, February 1966), 3.
8. Paul Dini, *Wonder Woman: Spirit of Truth* (New York: DC Comics, 2001), unpaged.
9. Personal correspondence from Jerry Siegel, November 21, 1987.

## Chapter 10 X-Men

1. Peter Sanderson, *The Marvel Universe* (New York: Harry N. Abrams, 1996), 213.

## Chapter 11 The Fantastic Four

1. Stan Lee, *Marvel Comics' The Fantastic Four* (New York: Pocket Books, 1977), 6.
2. Stan Lee, *Fantastic Four* #51 (New York: Marvel Comics, June 1966), 18.

## Chapter 12 The Punisher versus Green Arrow

1. *The Punisher*, produced by Robert Mark Kamen (Sydney, Australia: New World Pictures, 1990).

**H. Michael Brewer** is the father of two daughters and the husband of one wife—all strong and gifted women straight from a Chris Claremont comic script. He feels incredibly graced that these three super women have allowed him to hang around as their comical sidekick. ·

On the side, Mike is an adjunct professor of religious studies at Northern Kentucky University and a writer of sundry articles and books. Most of his writing is done in a room crammed with ten thousand comics, vintage paperbacks, CDs, autographed photos, original artwork, and various items he claims are rare collectibles. He is seldom interrupted while writing because sensible people are afraid to tread among the precarious piles in the "danger room."

Mike spends most of his time serving as pastor of Crescent Springs Presbyterian Church, where the worshippers make the best of sermons that draw on Spider-Man, *The Simpsons*, and classic Universal monster movies. Kids like to drop by his church study so they can play with his superhero action figures. After twenty-five years in the same congregation, most members have given up any expectations that Mike will outgrow this stuff.

A slow learner, Mike has spent much of his life in school collecting degrees, including a doctor of ministry from McCormick Seminary. He doesn't have any diplomas on his wall, but he has framed the certificates attesting to his baptism, his ordination, and his membership in the Merry Marvel Marching Society. He gives thanks daily that he can actually make a living flinging words into the world.